ESCAPE, BREATHE, IGNITE!

How to escape any rut.

ESCAPE, BREATHE, IGNITE!

How to escape any rut.

By Frankie Cote

Published by Be Infinity 2019

First Printing: 2019

ISBN: 9781793813466

Be Infinity
250 Yonge Street #2201
Toronto, Ontario, M5B 2L7

www.beinfinity.today

Ordering Information: Special discounts are available on quantity purchases by corporations, associations, educators, and others. For details, contact the publisher at:

frankie@beinfinity.today

I dedicate this book to my Dad, who showed me the value of fighting for what you believe in, my Mum who taught me how to love, my siblings with whom I've shared the great ups and downs of life and my wonderful, inspiring, and brilliant friends who have made my adventure possible.

Contents

Preface

In this book, you will learn how to escape any rut. By which, I simply mean that you will learn how to overcome any obstacle.

Sounds good, right? The best part, this isn't just hyperbole, I've overcome many huge ruts, so have many of my clients, and now, it's going to happen to you too.

I hear you ask, "How Frankie? Break it down for me!"

I'm glad you asked, because it couldn't be more straightforward. To achieve this, you will just need to learn and implement a simple framework I've constructed. A framework that is a product of ancient knowledge, personal experience, and simple science.

What I offer in these pages is a fresh perspective on something truly timeless. A way to not only understand ourselves, but also to create the rich lives that we all dream of.

You can use this framework to find meaning in your life, learn how to break through the walls standing in your way, and learn how to escape any rut you find yourself in.

Sound too brilliantly life-changing to be realistic? I have some great news. This process is not for a select few geniuses, nor is it solely for 60-hour-a-week working, smartly suited, highly motivated entrepreneurs (of course, they are very welcome as well!). This process can be applied by anyone and everyone, and best of all, it always starts with a rut!

Why is this such great news? Because we've all been in ruts at one point or another. We've all experienced those hours, days, months, and sometimes years, when life seems drained of all purpose. All of that wasted time we spent doing something we didn't like or being someone who just did not feel like 'us'.

We've all lived through, and continue to live through, times when we genuinely ask ourselves, "*How the hell did I get here?*".

We often find ourselves stuck, and, sometimes, we remain this way for so long that we even outright forget what a liberated life feels like.

"But how do I know if I'm in a rut Frankie?" I hear you ask.

Here are a few good signs that you may have fallen victim to a rut:

- Monday morning feels like a prison sentence or an insurmountable hill that you must climb.

- You spend most of your waking day working at a job you find so tedious, stressful, or soul-sapping that you catch yourself glancing at the clock every few minutes.

- You feel that by the time you get to do the things you really want to do every day, you are far too tired to do them.

- You have decided that the weekends are really the only time when you can be yourself, have fun, and live purposefully.

- You say things like "That's just the way things are for us grownups".

Does this sound a little familiar?

You wish for changes in your life more than anything else, but you can't seem to move on from that job that pays well but is as dull as ditchwater, or leave that relationship where you've coped with the fact you don't love your partner anymore, or maybe you wish to ditch those extra 60lbs you carry but just can't seem to stick to your diet plan.

You want to know how I know that? I've been there many times.

I mean, don't we all think, life is ok. This can go on a little longer. Change isn't too pressing an agenda. If you leave things long enough, perhaps they'll change of their own accord? All good things come to those who wait, right?

But what are you waiting for?

Admittedly, it's unlikely that the end of our world is near. But with each passing second, the end of our own human experience approaches ever closer. Tick, tick, tick. Just in reading those last three words, you are 3 seconds closer to death.

Scary eh?

Life is no dress rehearsal. We are all performing for the final time on the opening night. However many slip ups, the audience must have their resolution, and as we reach our theatrical climax, our final breath, we are often left wondering where the time went.

While we live, however, we have a simple choice to make. We can choose to submit to our fear and ceaselessly struggle in indifference. Or we can choose to live more soulfully realizing that every complication along our path has a lesson to teach us.

It's really that simple. We can suffer in the shadows of our own self-limiting perspective or learn life's lessons and become better people with every obstacle we overcome.

There's one thing for sure though, to get the best out of life, we must learn how to escape our personal traps, defeat the demons in our past, tackle our repressed emotion and step into the better 'us' we know we can become.

That is why I wrote this book.

So, how will this book work?

The book will take us through a simple framework which can be used to escape from any rut, a framework not dissimilar to that taught in my online course *'HOW TO TRANSFORM YOURSELF AND LIVE YOUR BEST LIFE'*. A framework I've used to change the lives of my coaching clients.

Over the 29 years I've spent on this planet, I've been many things, including:

- A successful performing artist, singing the songs I wrote in my bedroom as a teenager to crowds of 1400+ people, by the age of 21

- A daily radio presenter for a digital radio station and content creator for the UK national prison service radio station, with my mini documentary packages being heard by approximately 33,000 prisoners across the UK

- A Director of Strategic Partnerships at an advertising technology business firm, tasked with direct business growth

- A team player, closely making the cut, for an international amateur gay soccer team

- A care worker working one-to-one with severely autistic young adults – specifically, responsible for a young man with the mental age of a 6-month-old

- A poet – I once wrote 443 poems in 443 consecutive days and published them online

- A severe alcoholic on the verge of life threatening liver cirrhosis

- A drug user, who once 'bombed' ketamine and MDMA and then washed it down with a bottle of champagne

- Suicidal, with 2 failed attempts

- 140lbs overweight and utterly miserable

- A dreamer

These are to name only a few.

In short, I've worn many hats. Some which were good and some far from even ok.

Interestingly, every hat swap I've made started with an abrupt realization that I simply did not like the hat I was wearing anymore. If you're reading this then I assume you can relate.

Don't worry, I've got your back.

It's very important to accept that life is sometimes tough, with many difficult lessons to learn, and it's unrealistic to expect that we won't ever run into any rough patches.

Also, overcoming ruts is hard work, and I'll be the first to admit that I've reacted quite terribly to some of mine over the years. But what many people don't realize or fully appreciate is that ruts are actually beautiful lessons in disguise. Lessons that lead us to the answers that can resolve not only the problems we find ourselves trapped in but also relieve us of the burden of past suffering.

Lessons that will set us free.

Lessons are rarely easy to learn, especially when you're not entirely sure what they are, what they really mean, or why they're there. To further make things trickier, there is always the hard way to learn lessons, and then there's the easy way. Some of these lessons took me well over a decade to fully understand and learn from. I had to learn these the harder way.

I want to help you avoid learning lessons the hard way.

To escape a rut, we need a personal transformation. We must grow bigger than the rut. Transformation re-awoke within me a long dormant, totally natural, love for life, which I'd once known intuitively as a young child, before being disciplined on how to ignore it. Transformation taught me how to appreciate the simple pleasures, helped me develop greater gratitude and fortitude, and made me more aware of the wrongful notions that had been holding me back.

I am free, and you can be too.

As you haven't put this book down yet, I'm going to assume that you are ready to embark on this journey of change. So, let's dive straight in.

Best of Luck,

Frankie

Introduction

Throughout this book, I will be making references to concepts outlined in my *'HOW TO TRANSFORM YOUR-SELF AND LIVE YOUR BEST LIFE'* online course and coaching program of the same name.

Why?

To escape a rut one must grow bigger than it, and to achieve this we must go through a transformation. Ultimately, both resources point towards the same end.

After taking a close look at the many transformations I have been through, as well as the beautiful transformations of the people I've coached along the way, I soon realized that there were many repeating patterns of events, triggers, and choices that resided at the core of every successful transformation.

I then set about researching, reading extensively, and gathering information from the several wondrous fountains of abundant knowledge that exist all around us.

Once, I had combined these parts and broken them down to their elements, I was able to create a simple and effective framework that would facilitate the desired transformation. A transformation that would allow us to grow bigger than any rut. This framework, which is broken down into a triad of segments, can be used to expedite the process of breaking out of a rut, a process that could otherwise take an excruciatingly long time.

Let's be clear on one other thing too, I do not believe I have the exact answer to why you are in a rut, nor will this process tell you anything about yourself that you don't already know intuitively – in your beautiful core. Even if the answers to your problems remain quite unclear to you at this point, it is my fundamental belief that you already know who you are, what you need to do, and where you are heading, on a purely intuitive basis. You were born with knowledge of yourself, but this self-awareness has been blunted by all that you've 'learnt' since. The process outlined, my technique, is merely a tool to help you un-cover your personal truth, to expand your self-awareness, and to escape the ruts you're stuck in.

There are three key stages for transformation – ESCAPE, BREATHE & IGNITE. Here is a breakdown of each component.

STAGE 1 – ESCAPE

This stage is centred on gaining control of our thoughts, our health, and our time. In learning how to take control of our behaviour and habits in these three key areas, we are able to address key issues that are holding us back from achieving personal growth.

Taking control involves assuming a radical responsibility for where we are, what we have become, and where we are going next.

STAGE 2 – BREATHE

This stage focuses on exploring the life we led before we went off track, reconnecting with ourselves to get back on track and uncovering the little gem of wisdom we have attained through this experience.

This process involves a little backtracking, but it allows us to avoid major pitfalls in the future and also allows us to find peace.

STAGE 3 – IGNITE

This stage challenges us to set new and bold goals for our lives, teaches us how to express ourselves more authentically and shows us how we can celebrate life and express gratitude for the lessons we have learnt.

It is really as simple as that – three segments, each broken into three steps.

Let's get to work.

Chapter 1
Escaping our Mental Traps

September 2010, Portsmouth, England

The night was unlike any other.

Anticipation hung in the air, blending formlessly into the nauseating stench of beer, sweat, and the faintly bacon-tinged whiff from smoke machines.

I could taste the contents of my stomach at the back of my throat, as my photographer and long-term friend shouted, "They are hot man! You are going to kill it".

I am going to kill it!

I swallowed the bile.

I am.

As I stepped onto the stage, the roar of a 1400-strong crowd pierced straight through my nerves and inundated me with endorphins.

I was fulfilling a dream.

"Are you f*cking READY?" I bellowed out to the sea of faces in front me.

They roared even louder.

I was singing before the biggest crowd I had ever performed to, alongside a Number 1 artist on the UK chart. I was performing songs that I had lovingly composed, in the confines of my bedroom since my early teens.

The crowd swayed, roaring and arms flailing. I did too, pouring every last ounce of myself into the words that escaped my mouth like convicts released after being locked away in my chest for an eternity.

It felt magical, authentic, and deeply cathartic.

My faith had been repaid, my desires met, and my words, "I am a performer, I am worthy, I am a star", proved truthful. This was a clear, proud display of something that I had long known and believed to others around me. My inner truth was now an external experience.

The performance was over as swiftly as the batting of an eyelid.

With what seemed like just another blink, I was backstage with the crew, my friends and my stage partner.

I was beaming, a wide smile painted across my face.

Had you been there and asked me, "Hey, Frankie! How are you feeling?"

The reply would've been, "I'm feeling great, what an amazing show!"

I may have even high-fived you and offered you a drink, or twelve. I would have struck you to be a happy-go-lucky, party-loving, frontman of a band on its rise – a winner who was celebrating without a care in the world, happy to have just ticked off a major item on their bucket list.

But this couldn't have been farther from the truth. In fact, it was the ultimate deception.

In all honesty, **I felt dead inside.**

This show, in fact, took place only a few months before I made my first, of two, unsuccessful suicide attempts.

Behind a mesmerizing mask of charisma, my inner world was crumbling to pieces.

"But why?" You may have asked confused, had I let on that something was this horribly wrong.

All I had ever wanted, since I was a young teen, was to perform at a show just like the one I had stepped off the stage from. I had dreamt of it and worked tirelessly towards it without any financial assistance, without any formal network of industry peers. And with only my unassailable pep to back me, I had made this work.

So, what on earth was so terminal about my situation?

The shorter answer would be that the positive transformation I had experienced – the one that had made me the enigmatic singer of an electro-pop duo from being the shyest kid in class – had not been the only one that had occurred in the preceding years.

An equally powerful, far more devious, transformation had been simultaneously taking place. I had once been a healthy and happy young boy, but was, at that point, almost morbidly obese, dependant on alcohol and drugs, suffering from chronic anxiety, and struggling with suicidal thoughts and depression.

I had undergone two seismic transformations with two very different outcomes over the same five-year stretch.

One let me achieve a major dream, and the other made me want to end my life.

However different these situations were, there was one striking connection between the two. This similarity relates to the power of the mind, our subconscious and our ability to tell stories, which eventually become our reality.

The positive transformation began with a thought, a dream. A simple belief that if I worked tirelessly, my songs would eventually reach that big crowd of cheering fans that I envisioned. A belief that I had the potential to do a great deal in music, even though the bullying at school intensified as a result of my pursuit of this belief. My belief soon permeated the depths of my subconscious and became a part of my wiring. It became the story I would tell about myself. And in becoming a part of my fibre, I became a success in music even before I had performed my first show. I felt it before it was an objective reality. I told the story repeatedly, until it became a reality. I offered no resistance to this reality that was coming towards me, I just prepared as best as I could for the moment it would finally arrive.

The negative transformation in my life, which manifested itself in many insidious ways, but most visibly in the form of obesity, also began with a thought. Around the same time that I was regularly bullied at school for my early attempts at making music, I was also beginning to question my sexuality. Unfortunately for this particular line of inquiry, I was raised in an unforgiving and strict religious environment. The exploration of ones sexuality was simply not an option. As the cherry on top of this emotional 'crap-cake', I was also constantly running away from some childhood trauma.

Where I was strong and faithful in my desire to succeed as a musician, I was writing a far more destructive story for almost all other facets of my life. As a result, my fragile and broken mind became fertile soil for self-harming and addictive behaviour. It all began when I developed an emotional eating disorder and started packing on the pounds. A few months after this disorder took a hold of me, things became a lot worse.

One fateful day, my dad took me aside and said, "you're getting fat, what have you been eating?"

That word engraved itself upon my fragile mind, **fat.**

I remember the gut contorting shame that came moments after the initial sting of what could only be a taunt. The bullies were bringing down my morale, my strict religious upbringing was creating constant stress around my burgeoning sexuality, and now my dad was calling me fat!

Of course, he had only meant to help, and we have since discussed this, and he did apologize. But at that time, his words resonated in an all too familiar way. As a result of this familiarity, I didn't put up much resistance against the thought. I was used to feeling oppressed by others. I was used to letting others define my life in terms of everything other than music.

As a result of my weakened will, I started writing the first chapter of a truly destructive new story. Till then, I'd been living off only one book, '**I am a popstar**', but now, I was also dealing with a far less desirable book called '**I'm fat**.**

Soon, all I saw in the mirror was fat, although at this point I was far from it; at worst, I was only a little chubby. But it felt too late to change, and my perceived 'fatness' swiftly became a key narrative dictating my subconscious. Over time, I made compounding decisions that complimented this belief that I was fat and, as a result of this, I actually became fat.

Your mind is that powerful. What you believe to be true must materialize in your life, in one way or another. The important word here being believe, not want, not wish for. 'Believe'.

This simple dual example showcases the almighty power of our subconscious, a part of our being that scientists have barely scratched the surface of. The mind is a formidable asset, only as long as it is working in our favour. Should it start undermining us, it swiftly becomes a cage, from which we have to learn to escape.

But, how do we escape? By doing exactly that which got us trapped in the first place. By narrating a story.

We are all born storytellers. In fact, stories are the primary way in which we communicate with one another. Using language, we weave tales relating to the people we know, the objects around us, and we even use words to attempt explaining the intimate workings of our inner dialogue. We live to constantly learn through, share, and tell stories, whether about lessons learnt or just about Dave in accounting who broke up with his wife of ten years to date a girl half his age.

There are many types of stories we can tell, but in the end, they fall neatly into two brackets – those that spread love, and those that take it away. This is particularly clear when it comes to the grandest and most epic story we ever tell, the story of our lives.

We tell stories about ourselves all the time, and these stories aren't just innocent tales. As a matter of fact, they are formed from our experiences, opportunities, and success.

I told a story, that I was fat, and soon enough, I was. I told another story, that I was performing for big crowds of fans, and over time, it became true.

Strangely, many of us are never told that we can change the story about ourselves. Instead, we are told that we must settle and make do with the cards that we are dealt; that we must not rock the boat. We are advised to choose comfort over challenge, security over success, and convenience over freedom.

We are told to actively avoid excitement and adventure, and we happily do this, as we are driven by a fear that should we write something epic for ourselves, we will fail.

Adding to this bottomless confusion, are the endless stories we are told about ourselves by external sources. Should we not conform to societies newest interpretation of beauty, we are deemed unattractive. Should we interpret life differently than our culture dictates, we are deemed counter-culture.

We are being endlessly defined and re-defined by the ever-changing stories of society, our peers, and ourselves. The goalposts keep changing, and as a result, we are always left feeling like we've lost our various battles. This is how we end up in ruts. Our lives become a muddled mess of misguided self-belief, lofty societal expectations, and flawed decisions based on fear, that eventually lead to inevitable regret. Thankfully, this can all be undone.

It is of paramount importance, if not our strict duty, to honour our existence through persistent growth. We are here to dream of a beautiful, peaceful life, not to merely settle. We are here to shine with the unique beauty we all have. We are here to define ourselves, our lives, and here to take responsibility for our choices.

We are here to take control.

We are here to tell our own story and no longer allow it be told by others.

We are here to say *"I am"*, until it becomes so in our lives.

On the day I first thought of converting my transformational framework into a book, I proclaimed, *"I am a writer who's published a book to help countless people heal"*.

As you read these words, it has come to be.

It can be done. It will be done.

It starts today with you.

THE KEY TAKEAWAY

- We are all, always, recounting stories about ourselves. The happiness, success, and peace we create in our lives hinges on the good stories we tell about ourselves. The sadness, failure, and frustration are based on the negative ones.

- It is vital to understand and respect just how powerful your subconscious is in aiding, or rather destroying, the chances of living your dream life. The grandest stories, and even the most damaging lies, you tell yourself are all stored in the personal library in your head, your subconscious.

- When your subconscious isn't working in your favour, it is often working against you. When working against you, it will cause you many problems. But when working with you, it will help you achieve your greatest desires.

- Often, when you fall into a rut, your subconscious is working against you.

- Your subconscious can be trained to work for you. You can teach your subconscious certain thoughts or patterns of thinking, which when repeated enough become part of your story.

- A great way to begin training your subconscious is to ritualistically write affirmations. An affirmation written twice a day, every day, soon lodges itself in your subconscious mind and changes the way you think over time. The way you think, in turn, changes your actions. Through refreshed actions, we can radically alter the course our lives, in any direction as we please. This bestows us with the power to re-write our stories.

- The greatest affirmations of all start with two words, 'I am'. In saying these words, we start telling more positive stories about ourselves, stories that soon get lodged in our subconscious, stories that will come true with time should we keep telling them.

AN EASY START FOR TRAINING YOUR MIND

An easy practice to get into, to start training your subconscious mind, is to write daily affirmations. An affirmation is a repeated positive statement that will help you challenge pesky self-sabotaging thoughts. This process is something I cover extensively in my online course, *'HOW TO TRANSFORM YOURSELF AND LIVE YOUR BEST LIFE'.*

Over a relatively short period of time, you will start to subconsciously believe what you are telling yourself through a process known as auto-suggestion, which fundamentally alters your world view. By changing all your thoughts, you invariably impact your actions, and that changes your life. Here is a simple process for writing transformative affirmations:

Take a moment to think of something about yourself that you would like to improve or see changed in the future. *e.g. I don't like the fact that I get angry so easily.*

1. If you could wave a magic wand, and become a person that didn't have this problem, what would

be different? *e.g. I don't get angry. I react calmly when people irritate me.*

2. Write your affirmation (*remember: If you could wave a magic wand, and become a person that didn't have this problem, what would be different?*) from the perspective of the person you will be when you no longer have this problem. *e.g. I am calm, serene, and at peace. Anger may come to me, but I don't take it out on others, I simply let it go.*

3. With the repetition of this affirmation twice daily, this new story and belief embeds itself in your mind. The next time you find yourself in a situation that you can feel is making you angry, this new message in your wiring calms you down and makes you exit the scene of the unfolding drama before you get too angry. As a result, you are perceived as less angry, you lash out less frequently, and you are more peaceful. Simple, yet effective.

Once this affirmation is firmly lodged in your mind and becomes part of your fabric, you can move onto something else. Perhaps, you want to create something in your life instead of changing something you don't like. Be creative!

To note, if an affirmation seems unrealistic at this point, then consider writing a commitment instead. Commit yourself to changing something and when you start to see how it might be possible, start affirming it. Remember, we aren't trying to trick our brain, we are simply trying to redefine the way it interprets the world around us.

Chapter 2
Escaping our Health Traps

February 2005, Surrey, England

You must be perfectly quiet.

Not a single peep.

Creaaaaak!

The second last step of the staircase squealed on me, as I put my foot on it's cold, cheap carpeting. I froze.

Stay. Perfectly. Still.

My ears scanned silently for a sonic signal that I'd given away my location.

Did they hear me?

I heard the tuneless hum of our cheap kitchen fridge buzzing seamlessly over the laborious ticking of the clock on the kitchen's far wall. Tick, tick, tick. I took a deep breath and exhaled quietly, trying to calm my racing heartbeat till it tuned to the punctuated clicks of the timepiece.

The orchestral sting of the ten o'clock news' escaped from the lounge, where my parents would certainly be.

I'm in the clear and I'm right on schedule.

I tiptoed stealthily down the remaining steps, creeped through the hallway and into the kitchen, increasingly aware of how loud my breathing sounded. I glided slowly

19

towards the cupboard above the stove. Edging ever closer to the treasure trove of treats.

Floating in from the lounge, I heard the news presenter speaking with particular solemnity, "Breaking news on the developments in the US today".

I tiptoed closer to the cupboard.

"We go live to the scene . . ."

Almost there.

"Please be aware that some scenes may be disturbing, viewer discretion is advised".

As I climbed onto the counter, I heard my mum's voice from the other room. "This is absolutely dreadful", she sighed sadly. I didn't hear whether my dad responded, I was too focused on the task at hand.

I slowly pulled the door of the candy cupboard open and tentatively reached in, as if I were a bomb defusal expert, to extract my tasty treasure.

One wrong move, and they'll hear you. Don't mess this up!

I wrapped my hand around my prize and slid it out with the delicate touch of a surgeon. The TV continued to blare from the other room as I inched myself back down off the counter and hastily slunk away.

"The death toll continues to rise, and this is set to be the worst hurricane to ever hit New Orleans", the newscaster continued.

I got two bars today! Nice.

I heard my dad's voice as I skipped the creaky step on my way up, "What is the government doing?" He sounded exasperated.

Phase one of my plan was completed as I rounded the corner at the top of the stairs and switched on the bathroom light. I hurried inside to the cosy beach themed room, latched the little lock on the door, and plonked my ever-expanding butt on the closed toilet seat.

I need to be quick. What if one of them needs to pee?

Soon, I was hastily unwrapping the chocolate bars. Within moments, it seemed like I inhaled the first bar. Soon after, the second was gone as well.

Phase two was now complete, and onto phase three, the easiest one.

Wrappers in hand, I stooped down beside the old radiator by the shower. There was a little hole by the pipe that passed down through the floor, a builder's mistake, a gift to me. I shoved the used wrappers down my shameful hidey-hole.

And they were gone. I was done!

I made sure I flushed the toilet, before I headed back to bed. Just in case someone was out there listening.

I have to keep up the act.

Then, I slipped back into the bedroom I shared with my younger brother. He snored peacefully at its far end, and I quietly slid into my bed.

Now it was time to sleep. I closed my eyes, the sweet taste of chocolate still caressing my tongue.

I sighed and let my head sink into my pillow.

That was nice. You deserve nice things. You deserve a treat.

It's good to be nice to yourself, especially with all that shit going on. Right?

Yes. Everything is fine. Just sleep.

Well, no. It's not. Remember how you thought today would be different?

I roll over to my side.

They still laughed when they heard your song at school today.

You remember what they said?

The sweet taste on my tongue stings, slightly saccharine. I glance at the time. It's 22:23.

You deserve it though, you're a sick little sinful boy. You are broken.

Here we go again!

Dad said you're wrong. That means you're wrong. You're going to hell!

You will literally be tortured for all of eternity.

I felt sick.

But that wasn't a bad thing. Feeling sick meant I could sleep. It would give me something to focus on beyond the incessant chatter of my mind.

And for this, feeling sick became my friend.

I focused on the grumbling in my stomach and blocked out the bullying voices in my head.

Eventually, I fell asleep.

And that was my routine every single night, day after day.

A few months on, and many late-night runs later, my dad called me fat for the first time.

I recently asked my mum whether she had had any idea that I had been making late night runs to nick treats from the cupboard, back when I was in my early teens. I was sure she had been totally unaware.

She laughed and told me, " I didn't know until we refurbished the bathroom and pulled up the floorboards".

Oops.

As I had mentioned in the last chapter, since the day my mind started to believe I was fat, things started to seriously plummet. But it was not these thoughts alone that created the reality of me being fat. Thoughts independent from actions cannot materialize realities, they instead act more as empty wishes.

That said, the devious partnership between my thoughts and the actions triggered by them, primed me for some serious weight gain.

And boy, did that happen!

By the time I was in university, I was drinking something shy of an entire bottle of whisky a day. That was on a good day, and those were far outnumbered by the bad ones. I remember that on my best friends 21st birthday, all of us agreed to drink 21 alcoholic beverages each at a local club, the one with the questionable sticky floors but student friendly prices, as a means of celebrating. Oh, and there was another stipulation. These 21 drinks had to be downed within 3 hours before closing (this was after our pre-gaming during which I had already consumed my customary bottle of whisky). I was the only one to complete the challenge, and I'm told I pebble-dashed the street outside with my half-digested dinner as we left.

The excess alcohol helped me gain even more weight. This compounded with a diet that consisted mostly of salty, starchy, and oily hangover food caused some serious damage to my health. My daily dinner, at the time, was almost always a full pack of ten frankfurter sausages (fried), a bag of seasoned microwave rice (doused in the oil from the sausages), a splash of ketchup (liberally applied), and a great dollop of mayonnaise.

I was out of control and deeply ashamed of what I'd become. Every time I mistakenly caught my reflection staring back at me from a shop window, or a puddle, or on the back of a spoon, my whole body would experience a tremendous ripple of anxiety.

You fucking fat whale. You're pathetic.

l purposefully never looked at myself in a mirror. In fact, I got rid of the one in my room, and if I ever did catch an unplanned glimpse of myself in one, I would drink away the shame.

Drink, you fat fuck. No one will love you like this. May as well get wasted and forget that.

The drinking would lead to vile junk food, and the cycle was perpetuated with the utmost ease.

Although I was doing big shows and truly grateful for my progress in music, I couldn't be more ashamed of how I looked. I was the ultimate double act. One wildly excited and the other deeply depressed.

After a particularly intense hangover, something that happened once every fortnight or so, a little magic would occur. I would have a fleeting realization that I had the chance to change. I would be walking in the park or strumming my guitar or listening to music, and it would suddenly hit me.

You can change! It will be hard, but it's not impossible.

I channelled this sentiment into a song I wrote at the time, the lyrics are as follows:

'And we're floating so dangerously, close to the edge.
And we can fight it, but we'll never win.
Oh, it's a beautiful day, and I made it again,
And yes, I'm a mess, but I'm glad that I'm still alive'.

And I would try to change. From low carb to low fat, more fruit and more veg, fasting, running, gymming, giving up the frankfurter habit . . . I tried it all.

Nothing worked. So invariably, I always slumped back to my old ways.

After many pitiful and failed attempts to act on the reminders that I could change, my depression hit its lowest point. My life had become a toxic mess of my repressed sexuality, self-sabotage, and misery.

I had already made two suicide attempts. I came very close to jumping from a bridge over a motorway, and I also almost got crushed by a car as I lay in the middle of a road, at night.

I'd not planned on getting out alive on either occasion.

Incidentally, I was saved on both instances by simply fortuitous and somewhat incredible circumstances. I did not jump from the bridge due to a completely unexpected phone-call from my mum, which came just as I was climbing onto the barriers.

Just like a Hollywood movie.

When I later asked her what had prompted the call, she said, "I felt like something was wrong and I wanted to check if you were alright".

During my second attempt, the first car that rounded the corner as I lay in the middle of the road was a police car, which had been moving slowly on a night-time patrol. It's sufficient to say that the policemen were not impressed. They told me that if I didn't move from my resting position in the middle of the road, they would arrest me. It seems funny to think that at a time I was apparently ready to die, I absolutely did not, under any circumstance, want to get arrested.

After these two traumatic events, I was carted back home, where I stayed in bed for three months or so. Life had stopped entirely.

Then, a peculiar thing happened around the fourth month following my second failed attempt. Something unexpected. I'm still not entirely sure what triggered it, but drowning in my darkest turmoil, I suddenly saw one clear and simple truth.

I'd hit rock bottom, and I now had nothing left to lose.

I had little stopping me from being or doing whatever I wanted to, because I was nothing at that point. I felt like everything had already been lost, and that sense of completion was totally liberating. Plus, I was a survivor, and it was my duty to make something of the life I had. I realized then, that I may still be here for a reason. It wasn't my time to shine yet, not even close, because I hadn't accomplished a fraction of what I needed to.

But what do I need to do?

That night saw my first good night's sleep in years.

And then things clicked. The next day when my dad mentioned an opening for an unpaid radio producer role, at the prison he worked, I didn't say no.

Just like that, I had a new routine. I woke up at 5am, took the early commuter train into London, and spent time interviewing prisoners, learning about prison life, and slowly realizing that a lot of these men in prison were just normal people, who had lived through abnormal, and often deeply traumatic, circumstances.

Although I'm in no way attempting to justify their crimes, at that point, I was able to see beyond their past. To see them as they were at present. It helped me, because maybe just like them, one day, some people would see me differently from the wreck I had become. I found a glimmer of hope and some comfort in this thought.

I saw men whose lives were restricted to tiny, shared cramped cells. Men whose social time with each other was limited to a few hours a day. Men who were in segregation for week-long stretches, who did not have contact with a single other person for the entirety of this time. I felt, as the multiple doors locked behind me, a shred of what it may feel like to have no liberty. For many men, this would be the life they had for the next decade. 3652 days of the same routine, the same surroundings, the same disassociation from society, as well as the same lack of contact with loved ones.

Despite this, I found it remarkable that a large number of the men I spoke to seemed to be in better spirits than I was.

This jarred me. It made me feel completely ridiculous.

How can these guys be happier than me? What the fuck is wrong with me?!

I remember one man, in particular. We'll call him James. So, James spoke to me after I'd been watching some of the prisoners take part in a rehabilitative drama class. He said, "Whatever has hurt you, you can undo. You have to take responsibility though. It all starts with taking responsibility".

The words seemed particularly poignant, coming from a convict. What faith he had! He worked past his crimes, towards a better future.

To this day, I'm not sure how he had read me so clearly. I can only assume that he saw that I was in a state of considerable anguish. I think he could relate to it.

That night, something clicked. I realized that my attempts at losing weight and finding my healthy body had been too short term. Crash diets and intense 30-day gym programs were all quick fixes. What I really needed was a lifestyle overhaul. I needed something lasting. Something that would remain in place for the rest of my days. Something that would stop me from ever coming back to where I was.

And I knew it started with the mind, so I addressed that first.

I started telling myself a new story, one that replaced the tired old "I'm fat". I started saying to myself, "I am healthy, I am just wearing a suit of emotions that I can shed over time". With a little dedication and repetition, my mind picked up this affirmation and started repeating it to me.

With my mind now working for me, I started implementing small changes to my diet, lifestyle, and exercise regime every week. Small changes such as having eight frankfurters instead of ten, taking rest days when I didn't drink alcohol, or making sure that I ate at least one fruit or vegetable a day. Within a year, I had made 52 small tweaks and lost around 30lbs.

I said to my mum then, "The best version of me is sober and a vegan". I could feel it, but I certainly wasn't even close to being it yet.

This statement would have certainly seemed completely irrational to anyone who'd known my story thus far, but my mum just smiled and said, "You can do it".

I was challenging myself to become the person I wanted to be. I had a vision, and I had growing momentum working for me.

By then, I had left the prison radio role and was working as an educator and carer for severely autistic young adults, whilst moonlighting as a presenter of a daily independent music radio show. I was finally taking control of my career path.

Within the next 5 years, making around 210 further tweaks, I lost 140lbs.

Over those 5 years, I had also started to see my excess weight as a safety net protecting me from the unaddressed trauma in my past. So, I'd attended counselling, completed a course of intensive Cognitive Behavioural Therapy, and worked on myself every day in whatever way I could. This compounded with my health tweaks and new mantra gave rise to an unstoppable agent of positive change.

Without the tweaks, my mindset would have changed but my waistline may not have done so as dramatically.

I'm now a very healthy weight for my height. I am alcohol free, and I'm a vegan. Just like I had always wanted to be. This was all achieved with the help of tiny tweaks, and over time.

These small changes, which could seem meaningless at face value, in the end, helped me develop the body and lifestyle that I truly desired. It happened in the exact same way I'd put on the weight in the first place, only, this time, in reverse.

The tweaks can work in your favour, or they can work against you. When we are in a rut, we often allow minuscule negative habits, tiny negative tweaks that compound over time to become severe. Be they with our physical health, mental health, career, relationships, or any other facet of our lives, we can undo these over time, with small, regular positive tweaks.

As James had said in the prison courtyard after the rehabilitative drama, whatever has hurt you, you can undo. All you have to do is take responsibility though. It all starts with taking responsibility.

The biggest gift I received from implementing all these little tweaks with regard to my health, was that as I shed the weight, I was able to slip out of my suit of emotions. I confronted my repressed sexuality, accepted myself for my imperfections, forgave those who had hurt me (including myself), and learnt to speak openly about some of my darkest secrets and greatest shames, thereby diminishing their hold on me.

Now, I know that almost anything can be achieved in life, as long as we reprogram our minds to believe we can achieve it and then implement small, but consistent, tweaks along the way to ensure that we are working towards our goal every single day.

With the mind and body working together, there isn't much that can stand in our way.

THE KEY TAKEAWAY

- We should all pay attention to our physical health. Getting into a rut, we often lose track of our health. To recover from a rut, we must take control of our health.

- Improving our health involves reframing the way we think about ourselves and, then, implementing tweaks to help us become the new person we envisage.

- Tweaks in our lives should not be overcomplicated, nor should they be too challenging. For these to be effectively carried out in the long term, we must keep them small, and affect bigger change over time. Let's say you want to kick out your coffee habit. Instead of cutting out coffee entirely straight away, why not just have two cups a day as opposed to three? Then, further down the line, make it one, then switch to decaf before losing it entirely. The tweak must be something that you can consistently maintain as your default choice. For good! (maybe minus a few rare occasions when you treat yourself)

- Just one tweak a week, over the duration of a year, accomplishes 52 little wins for our health. You are literally 52 times healthier than you were at the beginning.

- Have patience. Tweaks require time to work. But know that if you are consistent, within the first 8 weeks, you will start to see real progress.

- The tweak system is not just for our physical health, it can help us improve any facet of our lives, when properly implemented.

AN EASY START TO TWEAKING YOUR HEALTH

An easy practice to initiate to start tweaking your health consistently, is to keep a tweak list. This is a process I've honed with many clients and I cover in my online course *'HOW TO TRANSFORM YOURSELF AND LIVE YOUR BEST LIFE',* This list can be written on a piece of paper and stuck on your fridge, or noted on your phone or calendar, or any other place that you look at every day.

The process of tweaking your health, using a tweak list, is very simple. The purpose of the tweak list it to keep track of all the tweaks that you've implemented. Starting with Week 1 and Tweak 1, and ending at Week 52 and Tweak 52. Each new tweak is added to the current tweaks, and with each new addition, you become just that much healthier.

For example, here is a tweak list for the first 3 weeks.

Week 1) I will drink one glass of water when I wake up.
Week 2) I will eat a banana every day.
Week 3) I will do 5 squats every day.

It's important to keep these tweaks simple. You don't need to make them too challenging, nor overcomplicate them. We're here to make lasting change. For lasting change, these tweaks must be manageable.

It's also worth noting that the first 10 tweaks should aim at adding healthy habits into your routine and not focus on removing unhealthy ones yet. Once we have built up the confidence, routine, and strength to do so, we can tackle the unhealthier habits. We will want to by then. We will be motivated by the success we have already seen.

Simple and highly effective.

Chapter 3
Escaping our Time Traps

June 2006, Surrey, England

The day I last saw my grandad alive had been one I spent struggling to work through my junior level 'Extra Physics' homework. The 'Extra' classes were taught after school to students who showed potential in Science or Math. As the least promising of the selected students, I hadn't been pushed too hard to take this task on. Had I listened to my heart, I wouldn't have in the first place. But I was perpetually in a point-scoring battle with my brother, and doing an 'Extra' class would be something to brag about. Not that I could compete, he was far more able at Math and Science than I ever was.

I'll be honest here, I hated physics.

Granddad had been sick. That day, I'd been holed up in the guest bedroom at my grandparents' house. It had deep yellow walls that ill-fittingly housed a rickety bunkbed with jungle-themed sheets, a small work space, and a collection of assorted trinkets. The slightly stuffy air in the room was tinged with the synthetic scent of white musk, and had you opened the window to let it escape, you could have seen the garden. A garden that had always been well looked after by my grandad and his green fingers.

And then, I sat, silently, attempting to probe the recesses of my memory for the formula to calculate momentum.

Velocity multiplied by mass? Or divided?

And then, a knock on the door offered sweet temporary relief from my mental drill. It was my mum.

I remember how her mournful spirit had further drained the walls of their colour, as she had entered to tell me it was time to say goodbye to my grandad.

I've never said goodbye to someone for good before.

Her words have been forever emblazoned in my mind, "he doesn't have much time, you should come and say goodbye".

He had been diagnosed with a terminal disease, 3 years earlier. Remarkably, at that time, they had given him only a matter of weeks to live. But, he had fought hard, and in our eyes, he had won. He had made that extra time for himself, against all odds, to do what he needed to.

I followed my mum obediently into the room.

There was a solemnity in the air shared by everyone apart from my grandad, who seemed perfectly at peace and was breathing very softly. Close to his head, my Aunt's new puppy examined the adjacent pillow zealously. Near death and new life making peculiarly poignant bedfellows. I remember wondering whether my grandad's soul would find its way into the puppy's body when he died, as it left his body. Perhaps then, when everyone left the room, the puppy would walk up to me and say something like, "it's all ok, I'm still here".

I had recently watched a tv show where this had happened. It however seemed as implausible as me acing my upcoming physics exams.

I said goodbye to my grandad that day and told him I loved him. He had not really responded. I remember feeling I was kissing a waxwork dummy, as I had kissed his forehead.

And then, I left the room to return to my revision.

He died some time later, completely at peace, having seen all of his family.

It wasn't till a few days later that I was able to return to the room. The arrangements had been made, and the mourning had begun.

I remember a sense of apprehension as I stepped closer to the room he had died in, as if someone was hiding in there.

I stepped in through the doorway, hesitantly.

His body had been removed, the sheets had been changed, and for all intents and purposes, it was over. He was dead. He was gone.

But something kept me in that room, a sensation that seemed somewhat impossible to place, until I finally realized what it was.

I could feel him. And this wasn't a sensation akin to being watched, nor one that was based on any of my five senses. This was a feeling that resonated at my core.

He was still there. The part that had loved me. The part that had taken me to see the rugby team he used to play for. The part that had hidden candy in the glove compartment of his car to sneak onto our palms when no-one was looking. The part of him that had most deeply impacted me.

It wasn't gone. Not one bit.

It felt magical.

It would be another week or so before I went back to that room.

What was most extraordinary, when I wandered into the room expecting the same warmth I had experienced on that fateful day, it was gone.

The room was void of any energy. It was just an empty room again.

My grandad had afforded me my first true experience of spiritual clarity. He had stuck around, just long enough, to reassure me that he wasn't truly gone. He had made time for me, allowed me to process the experience, and moved on when he knew his point had been conveyed. No sooner, no later, nor when he was 'supposed' to. Just like he had always done. He had made time for what mattered most, even at the end.

Through this simple, final gesture, which remains quite unbelievable to many people I recount the incident to, my grandad taught me a beautiful lesson. He had proven to me beyond doubt that the love we share with others is our one true legacy in life.

We find love within ourselves and spend a lifetime trying to pass it on.

My grandad had always been an avid bird watcher, and he had spent much of his life trying to spot a kingfisher at a local lake. He had not succeeded to do so before he died. A few months after his death, we went on a family picnic to the lake he had loved. On that day, we saw the deep rich blue and fiery red brilliance of the majestic common kingfisher.

Beyond the gift of this insight into something infinite, I also had a stark reminder. Watching my grandad's three-year successful combat and eventual succumbing to terminal illness, I learnt that we cannot control when we leave this world, but we can choose to live with purpose for the days we have left. However many they may be.

My grandad's death also made me realize that it is of utmost importance to properly use our time, every single day.

Let's keep this simple. If you live to the age of 75, then you have spent 27,375 days on this planet.

That may seem like a lot at first glance, but if you are a 20-year old reading this, 7300 days have already elapsed.

If you are 30, 10,950 are gone. And if you are 40, 14,6000 of these 27,375 days have been spent.

This is of course assuming that you live to see 75, which is ultimately out of our control.

Seeing my Grandad's struggle with the terminal disease, his strength and his dignity made me uncomfortably aware of the time that I had been wasting. Over time, being able to identify wasted opportunities has become one of my greatest assets. It has allowed me the freedom to take risks, dive headlong into new challenges, and choose to live a life of abundance and happiness.

But it hadn't always been this way.

For many years, as I struggled through my darker periods, this sense of time-wasting became a constant source of anxiety. I was soon cripplingly impatient, I didn't want to waste a single second, and every moment spent doing something that didn't feel 'right' left me in a panic-stricken mode.

When I was spending time working on building a career, I felt as though I was wasting time that I should spend being joyful with my friends. After all, this could be my last day!

When I spent time with my friends, I felt like I was wasting time that could be better spent working on projects of my passion. After all, If I don't wake up tomorrow, what beautiful art will be displayed at my funeral.

When I was working on music and art, I worried I would never build a sustainable career. This was no way to make a living! I could be here another 50 years. What am I doing? I need to focus on building a proper career.

So, I'd work on my career and then feel as though I had no social time. This cycle of self-doubt and confusion surged through my head every passing moment of every single day, and I ended up hating everything I did. It was vicious, unforgiving, and a truly harmful interpretation that I made of my grandad's beautiful lesson.

Eventually, I sought help to deal with my chronic anxiety disorder. This was also when I confronted my mind and started implementing tweaks to my health.

Until eventually, when I fully overcame my anxiety, with the aid of extensive cognitive behavioural therapy, this dislike of wasting time was truly crippling. However, once overcome, it allowed me to be far more prescriptive about how I allocated my time.

I'd found another glimmering gem of truth by facing my self-destructive anxiety. Wasting time is not possible when you are both focused on improving your time allocation every day and being more mindful and attentive of completing all tasks, whether mundane or mind-blowing.

As long as I was working at improving my schedule every day, I wasn't wasting time. As long as I was focused on bringing all of myself to every task I did, I wasn't wasting time. Even if I was just washing the dishes, as long as

43

I focused intently on the process and on doing a good job, then that effort would be reflected in my life elsewhere. How I approached one task would be how I approached all. So, I'd better focus on being the best I can with every little thing I did.

I started to tweak my schedule, to allow myself the time to properly focus on my passions. An extra 20 minutes here and there, a bit of extra time to focus on the things I love.

I made 20 minutes every few days to listen to an inspiring piece of music or motivational speech. I cleared 20 minutes every week to go for a mindless walk to nowhere. I found 20 minutes every month to stop and think, to slow down, and eventually, to meditate.

I then realized that I could also improve on my time-wasting by adding in tasks that weren't as immediately enjoyable but would reap longer term rewards. I took 20 minutes a few times a week to workout. I found 20 minutes a day to properly brush my teeth (in my darker years, I had fallen out of this habit – I know, gross!). I made 20 minutes to read about topics that scared me. Say, finance.

With time, the small changes transformed into bigger ones. I liberated a huge amount of time by leaving alcohol and giving up my party lifestyle. This change alone afforded me around 21 extra hours a week.

My good scheduling choices compounded over time and these, alongside the tweaks to my health and the new stories I read to myself, allowed me to transform my life for the better.

With this new lighter headspace, when my career at a media company in London came to an abrupt end, I swiftly decided that I was ready for a major change. I was craving another leap of faith. I left London and my daily three-hour train commute to work, moving to Toronto where I only needed a twenty-minute longboard ride to reach the office from home.

In Canada, I spent two years working on my agenda to create more time for myself. I rescheduled my life to ensure that my days were filled with more and more of the activities I enjoyed. More and more of the people I loved. And more and more opportunities that make me feel alive.

Eventually I left my corporate career entirely and freed up a huge segment of time to work on more personally meaningful projects, connect with people, and kick-start my own life, on my terms. I now live as per my own time constraints. I march to the beat of my own drum.

It was just five years ago, I had no time all. Between work, partying, and the physical ramifications of my unhealthy lifestyle, I had only a few moments daily that were truly my own. I spent almost all of those moments sleeping, and when I wasn't sleeping, I was whining about how little time I had.

Most people spend their entire human experience bemoaning the fact that they just don't have the time to do what they truly want. That, or they defer the liberation of their time to retirement. A time when they are well past their youth and usually held back from taking risks due to family and fragile finances. A time that they may never even reach.

Don't make the same mistake. Assuming you will live to the age of 75, and I certainly hope you do, then on the day you were born, you had 27,375 chances to wake up one day and say, "This is it! I'm taking back control of my time".

How many days do you have left now?

The day I stopped moaning and started doing was a day like any other. In all honesty, it didn't initially feel like much was moving. I can promise you though, as I write these words, I am very grateful to my past self for having the strength to persevere. I'm proud of my journey.

Grandad is proud of my journey.

THE KEY TAKEAWAY

- We can all improve our lives by allotting a regular time to do the things we love. We only have a limited amount of time left, of which we may have even less-er than we hope. So, delaying our wish to enjoy life and explore new challenges is simply not an option.

- When transforming ourselves and escaping ruts, it is important to reconnect with activities that make us smile, make us stronger, or help grow our willpower. In doing so, we can remind ourselves of our passions, our interests, and our purpose.

- Just 20 minutes a day spent doing something we love adds up to 122 hours a year, 122 hours dedicated to something we truly enjoy.

- We will never again have more time than we do today. It is important to realize that overcoming a rut, as well as transforming ourselves and building our best life will take time, and unless we start today, we may never have a chance to succeed at this en-deavour.

- If you live to the age of 75, then you will have 27,375 days on this planet. At this moment, how many do you have left? How many more chances will you have to do what you love?

AN EASY START TO MAKE MORE USE OF YOUR TIME

An easy practice to get into, when trying to make better use of your time, is to inculcate an exciting 20-minute activity every day. This time is your time, a time dedicated to doing something that makes you smile, makes you stronger, or helps grow your willpower.

Once again, I cover this in depth during my online course. But here is an easy and quick process to uncover and establish your first new activity.

1) Ask yourself – what activity, that currently isn't in your daily routine, makes you smile and you wish you could do more of?

e.g. Singing out loud, writing poetry, or solving mind-bending puzzles

2) Ask yourself – when can I slice out 20 minutes from my day to focus on this activity that makes me happy?

e.g. I will take out 20 minutes after I get back from work and before dinner, or I will slice out 20 minutes over lunchtime.

3) Ask yourself – how will I hold myself accountable? How will I ensure that I do not skip these 20 minutes daily?

e.g. I will ask my partner to remind me every day, or I will leave a note on the TV that reminds me to do this activity before I relax for the night.

Chapter 4
Breathe in and Take it back to the Start

June 1995, Montreal, Canada

The king of the lions had ordered us to scour the Savannah with him in search of food, and it had always been advisable to heed the commanding words of the king.

He was the largest and eldest of the pack, thus, the leader. Under the influence of his almighty power, all other beings in the kingdom fell into line. This included his two little lion cubs. The younger of the two roared through baby teeth, and the elder, otherwise known as Frankie, was the one who would one day gain dominion over the pride lands.

My paws hit the living rooms hardwood floor haphazardly as I crawled behind my dad and younger brother. We were playing the game we loved the most.

In the next room, my mum hummed to herself as she boiled frankfurter sausages. Hot dogs were always a summer treat. My absolute favourite.

As we explored the wilderness, the soundtrack of the recently released 'Lion King' played out from our nearly ancient cassette player. This player was the highlight of a room otherwise decorated with limited upholstery, fur-

51

niture, or fittings. It alone could not combat the pervasive scent of poverty. In uproarious denial of the impoverished interior, the music was elegant. It gripped my attention, its beauty only accented by the infrequent roars of the king of the lions.

I feel loved.

I let out as mighty a roar as I could muster to indicate that I'd found something. My dad and brother came to investigate. We growled at each other, and I gestured towards the kitchen. I'd picked up a scent, and I was on the hunt. The lion king soon outpaced me as we scampered towards our lunch.

I rounded the corner at the exact moment that my Mum called out, "Hun, the hot dogs are read . . .' She saw me on the floor and stopped mid-sentence. She smiled and suddenly the savannah was gone. Instantly evaporated, just by the thought of our special summer treat.

The symphony from the other room provided an epic soundtrack as we feasted.

Fast-forward 22 years, and I'm sitting in a weekly sales projection meeting, idly counting the amount of times my colleague says 'umm' nervously, whilst delivering a somewhat mediocre hunting plan for the next quarter.

"And the direct accounts are set to grow . . . umm", that is number 23, "by umm (24)", she says, almost on her edge.

I glance at the time, just one solitary minute has elapsed since I last checked. I begin to question whether time is behaving in its typical manner, it seems to be standing completely and utterly still.

I glance out of the large window at the far end of the boardroom, just in time to see a plane pierce the sky with sharp white precision.

Perhaps this room is in a time warp?

"and things are looking far more positive for March . . . umm (25)", she continues.

I sigh absentmindedly, it slips out a little louder than planned, and I feel a tinge of embarrassment as I adjust myself on the seat. I guess no one heard.

What shall I have for dinner?

Suddenly, a sound from outside the boardroom grabs my attention.

Music! Familiar music at that.

"Then April umm . . . (26)"

It's from that movie I loved as a kid. Why is that playing here?

A wave of nostalgic warmth washes over my body.

It's that track! The one I really loved.

And then, it was gone, just as quickly as it had come. Someone had clearly been messing around with the office sound system, they were subsequently reprimanded for their impromptu DJ moment, and now tedious normality ensued once more.

But the warmth it left tingled in my bones. Soon, I started listening to that song daily. I felt as if it was trying to tell me something. What that was, I was unsure. This was until I remembered the lion game. The simplicity, the joy, and the freedom of those quieter times.

I was reminded of how liberated I had felt as a child. This soon developed into a nagging sense that I had lost something important, from deep within my core. I needed to somehow try and regain my freedom. I supposed, at that point, that there was more to life than logging in, working, and then logging out. I realized that re-discovering the freedom of youth was not only an aspiration, but a necessity, one that would bring lasting meaning to my life.

I don't want to sit smartly in this boardroom, I want to crawl on the floor and pretend I'm a lion!

It wasn't long before every perk I'd so willingly enjoyed in my corporate career previously seemed duller. The shine of glamour washed out by the greyscale grasp of my lacking freedom.

I had reconnected with what I was like at the start, and that made me realize how far off the track I had reached. I had entered the corporate world with two intentions. Firstly, to prove to myself that I could thrive in this space, and secondly, to pay off my student debt and build a stable platform from which I could easily leap back to the projects I loved. A whole year had elapsed since I'd paid off the last of my debt, and this was possible due to a big commission cheque I received for thriving at my job. The credits should have already been rolling on this particular episode of my life, yet I was still here, long after the final punchline had been delivered. My bright cheerful comedy had become a brooding drama.

I was one year late, and I could feel it now more than ever.

Although I had continued to learn, improved my health, and tweaked my life, something fundamental was missing. I was hollow, off track, and felt purposeless. If you asked my ex to describe what I was like at that time, he would say something along the lines of "a little lost and quite agitated". He's a very generous and kind guy, any other person would have said I was "a nightmare, constantly on a pursuit to find meaning but never finding it". It was common for me to pace around my swanky rented downtown condo at 2 am, muttering about how I was "so close to the next step".

Being reminded of the lion game, that was the breakthrough trigger.

Within 4 months of hearing the song, I quit my job, downsized my accommodation, and donated half of my clothes to charity. I was desperate to once more feel the childlike sense of liberation and peace that I had lost.

Within 5 months, I was living a fully stripped-down life that allowed me to make an impromptu trip to Europe. I saw my family in London, my old friends across the UK, and took some time off and went to the Netherlands to reconnect with myself.

Within 6 months, I was learning again, reading two books a week, exercising hard every single day, pursuing a more fulfilling career path, and making music that I couldn't have possibly even considered writing when I was trapped in any of my previous selves.

I am now grateful for this life, at peace with myself. And although life throws incessant challenges our way, both little and large, I now know that everything will be ok in the end. It's only a matter of perspective, our perspectives shape our reality. As long as I remain authentic, honest, and open, the right answer will always reveal itself when the time is right.

At one point between our childhood and our ultimate demise, we 'grow up', load ourselves with responsibility, enter the 'adult world', and we give up our freedom.

In return for relinquishing our freedom, we expect financial comfort, relative security, and entertainment. Lots and lots of entertainment.

But what is the meaning of a life spent doing a job you hate? A life so swarmed with drudgeries that you must placate yourself with entertainment and other assorted vices? Is a life of safe boredom really what we should strive for?

I realized soon after I left my job that I would rather be homeless and pursuing my dreams than be a millionaire who has given up on himself. Connecting with my authentic core, as well as what I was like at the beginning, helped me realize this.

Oftentimes, in relinquishing our personal freedom, we also surreptitiously release key parts of who we were at the start. In 'growing up', I lost touch with my sense of playful freedom, I lost my ability to properly connect with myself through music and art, and as a result, I lost a lot of joy in my life.

In tracing things back to the beginning, stimulated by a musical reminder from my past, I reconnected with myself, the real me.

You can and should do this too.

THE KEY TAKEAWAY

- We can all reconnect with what we were like at the beginning, and during a rut, this is a particularly useful thing to do. In doing so, we can better trace where we went off track. Equally, should we be looking to live our best life, we must be operating at a higher level, a level that we can only access after being unburdened of our 'adult' misconceptions of life.

- Our intuition can tell us if we are on the right track. If we hate Mondays, then it's very likely that we aren't on our best path. Unless there is a clear and concise reason that justifies what we are doing, we've probably just fallen into it and are staying put, as it's easier to do so than changing our path to pursue our best life.

- We can be mindful of what we are missing and take active steps to try and find out. Simple meditation techniques can be used to help us look back and try and understand where we may have lost our way.

- If you have absolutely no idea what to do with your life, know that trying something new, even if it becomes clear that it's not going to be something you enjoy in the long term, allows you to see life from an entirely different perspective. Through this fresh perspective, we can reconnect more easily with what we were at the start.

AN EASY START TO RECONNECTING WITH WHAT WE WERE LIKE AT THE START

An easy practice to begin with, when trying to reconnect with what we were like at the start, is to go through the following simple meditative exercise. This given time to reconnect with yourself can reveal simple truths about where you may have lost track of your life. There are three simple steps to this exercise:

1. Gift yourself 10 minutes and find a quiet place to sit or lie down. Ensure that you are in a comfortable position. Take a few deep breaths. Once you are considerably relaxed, close your eyes and imagine yourself as a child. See yourself as you were back then. Then ask the younger you, what do you love to do? If this does not have the desired effect, then regress back to the last time you remember laughing out loud, or smiling, or even feeling a rush of excitement. What were you doing? Why was it so enjoyable?

2. When you've returned from your thought exercise, plan the new action you will take based on what you've learnt about yourself. What new activity can you pursue from this new information? What tweaks can you make to your schedule to let yourself enjoy life a little more?

3. If you didn't 'hear' anything while meditating, DON'T WORRY. Just take time to repeat Step 1 weekly until something becomes clear. There is no rush.

Chapter 5
Breathe in and Get back on Track

December 2015, London, England

"We're letting you go", he said dutifully, that perpetual smile on his face briefly dimmed.

The words pierced through my chest and left a dead-weight on my stomach.

Fuck.

"It's not really you, it's more that we can see you aren't happy", he continued, giving me ample time to respond, however knowing it was unlikely that I would.

I'm not, but maybe I could be? Maybe I could change? I will care again! I promise.

The words did not actually leave my mouth. I had run out of the willpower to pretend any longer.

"We'll give you three months' pay, and you can leave today. Take this time to think through what you really want", he said politely, and that was that. I walked out of the boardroom for the last time. The glass door swung shut behind me, ending an era. I stepped out to the un-known.

The funniest thing, especially considering my shock, was that I knew this was coming all along. Not solely because I was visibly unhappy in the workplace, but also because I'd indirectly asked them to let me go. They were just doing what I'd asked. Yet, my mind raged against me.

Why did I want this? I'm so stupid. What am I going to do now?

I ignored their commiserating looks as I packed my belongings hastily. I saw my desk for all its ergonomic beauty for the first time, as I emptied the drawers. The office seemed more vibrant and joyful than usual as I shut down my computer for the last time.

Look at this great thing you are walking away from. It's not too late, go back and beg!

Ignoring my mind's imploring and following my heart, I scurried out into the night, hoping no one would see me.

Get away. Just get away. You're getting what you asked for.

As I paced the all-too-familiar walk through London, I felt deeply compelled to do two things, drink all the alcohol in the world and call my mum. I decided that the latter would be far more productive than the former.

Wow, I've grown. Drinking would always come first earlier.

I called her, feeling the damp chill of winter wind against my hand as it dialled – ring ring, ring ring.

"Hello", she said, friendly as usual.

I fully explained the situation to her and then the line seemed to go quiet for a moment as she thought. I navigated through a safe passage between a double decker bus and a speeding bicycle.

She finally broke her silence as I successfully crossed the road, "Well, this could be the best thing that ever happens to you", she was musing.

"I know", I retorted. Petulant about the truth. "It's just . . .', I continued, but I left the sentence incomplete.

"That you didn't think it would happen like this?" she suggested.

"Exactly! But, I did know that this was coming . . . and they gave me a very generous package".

"What will you do now?" she asked, steering my thoughts like a skilled sailor.

"I don't know". *Sigh.*

I really don't.

"You will", she told me supportively, "just give it a little time".

That was the end of that conversation, and I continued on to climb up the crowded steps of the Waterloo train station, wallowing in self-pity. I was drowning in emotion and bathing in the almost familiar dread of impending change. There seemed to be more people at the station than usual, or at least, they sounded much louder. I slid my way through the bustling crowd towards the announcement board where my train time and platform would be presented. I was interrupted by the huge speakers at the station before I could reach the board.

'Platform 9 for the 18:57 South-West Train service to Woking . . .'

That's me.

As a small human pack shunted away from the larger herd, I slipped my hand into my pocket to grab my ticket. I made a dash for Platform 9. By the time I reached the platform, my heart was racing, knees aching, and my mind had settled a little, but my mother's words continued to echo.

What will you do now?

I walked the length of the train in search of a seat and soon realized that I would be standing for the entire journey. By the time the train was on its way, I had been squeezed into a corner like a sardine in a can. This would normally have irritated me, but I was far too fixated on the future.

What WILL I do?

The train left the station late, the same way it always did, and I peeked out of the bit of window not obscured by the myriad of arms, shoulders, and heads between me and it's scratched pane.

Through it, I saw the drab, listless, and uninspiring urban sprawl. I saw my past, my misery, and little hope of opportunity.

Then, my stream of consciousness was broken by an announcement from the guard.

'Welcome aboard this South West Train Service to Woking, calling at...'

I phased out the familiar message and dove back into my thoughts.

All around me, the miserable commuting masses placated themselves with their addictive devices. They shuffled against each other like leaves disturbed by a gust, as the train swayed inconsiderately. The air was largely stale, accented only by the infrequent saccharine sweetness of cheap perfume and the far more frequent whiff of body odour. Then a lady, in a sharp business suit, whose shoulder had recently become closely acquainted with mine, peeled an orange, and its zesty spray offered me a few moments of nasal reprieve.

This was a train ride like any other. There was not a single remarkable thing happening beyond my thoughts. Life was trudging on as the masses suffered through the monotony of their daily commute. But unlike every other person on the train, the memory of this trip has not been relegated to the haze beyond my conscious mind. This was a trip I would never forget.

It was on this fateful trip home, crushed in the corner of a train carriage, trying not to press the emergency stop lever mistakenly, that I admitted that I'd lost track. I had stayed in my job so long that I'd grown to profoundly dislike it. I had stayed on in the UK, even though I could feel I belonged elsewhere in the world. I had changed very little in my personal routine of late and was lamenting the fact that I had made no new and inspiring friends. I had slowed down my health regime and was bitter that I wasn't losing weight. I was anxious about finding more meaning in my life, yet not acting on this sensation, merely sitting with it.

How the hell did I end up here? And how do I move along to something better?

I had well and truly lost track, I was in a big rut, and I was in need of a serious change. This had to be a major adjustment, something bold. It wasn't time to be restrained in my efforts. I'd ignored enough signs, I'd already lost too much of the joy in my life, and I had distanced myself from whatever I was here to do.

Some 40 minutes passed as I questioned my choices and attempted to mentally reframe my reality. Then, as I stepped off the train, onto the platform, back into the damp drizzle of southern England, I decided to move to another country.

That's bold enough, right?

I was sick of the commute, I was sick of the weather, and most of all, I was sick of my life there.

So I did.

A month later, I was speaking with a recruiter in Toronto and researching downtown flats (learnt that they are called condo's). Two months later, I was convincing my then partner to take the leap of faith with me. Three months later, we were visiting Toronto for an exploratory trip. Four months later, I was packing up my belongings. And five months later, I finally landed at the Pearson International Airport with all my belongings, packed in a backpack and a large suitcase.

This was one in a growing line of small to big leaps of faith I have taken in my life. A challenge to myself to make something better than what I had. A promise that life would be better, should I take that risk in search of the reward.

The universe, you see, has a funny way of pushing us where we need to go, regardless of our conscious preparedness. As long as we accept its influence, we will be guided to our deeper purpose and meaning eventually. As long as we are aware that there is a purpose and meaning, the universe will be resilient in its attempts to help us find it. Even if we ignore its many calls, it will eventually push us hard enough that we have to leap into the unknown.

Moving to Toronto was necessary for my story to progress. Toronto was the city where I was finally able to fully accept and explore my gender and sexuality, the city where I was finally able to forgive all the family members who had hurt me the most, and it was the city where I gathered the strength to take my next big leap of faith, out of the corporate world.

Had I not taken the leap of faith into the unknown, my life would have remained stagnant, and I would have remained miserable.

Toronto was also where I released my glut of excess emotional garbage, finally let it go. Although Toronto remains a city where I feel very comfortable, it is not actually Toronto that made this change possible. This could have happened anywhere in the world. Just as long as it was somewhere far enough from home to prove to myself, and the universe, that I was ready to take on the next chapter of my life.

We carry our pain around everywhere as if it were a heavy backpack. When I travelled from the UK to Canada, I did not only bring my limited belongings, I also travelled with my equally heavy but totally invisible emotional backpack.

Moving to Toronto was only possible due to the emotional unpacking I had done in the years preceding the move, and since moving, I was rewarded with the opportunity to dig deeper into the bag to pick up, examine, and release more of the pain I had been carrying. Prior to my move, I had unpacked the worst of my repressed sexuality, worked through the anger I'd felt in the past, and examined why I was still feeling fat – even though I was now of a far healthier weight and consistently on track towards my goals.

Just this little self-help had been enough to show me that I was ready for the next chapter, and the seed of moving to Canada had actually been planted in my mind around 6 months before the day I was let go. Since that day, here's how most conversations I had with anyone about my future sounded like, in script form:

Gemma from Marketing: It seems like you are in a bit of a rut.

Me: Yer, I'm working so hard at making changes in my life and trying to understand what I need to do. I'm doing so much better than before. I've grown so much. But there's always something missing, something I can't seem to put my finger on. I'm . . . I'm one inch away from the answer. But that inch is impossible to cover and the answer is impossible to see from where I stand.

Gemma from Marketing: Is there nothing that stands out when you think about what you want to do? Any indication of what may be hidden beyond that inch? Any potential routes you can walk down to try and find the answer?

Me: Not really, well . . . I do have one little thought.

Gemma from Marketing: Well?

Me: I have this little part of me that thinks I need to move base, and this even tinier part that says it should be Canada.

Gemma from Marketing: That's amazing! Why don't you? Like, what's stopping you?

Me: Well . . .

I would then spurt out a barrage of excuses, ranging from my finances to the weather, from my relationship to my career plans, and from my family to my political stance. My mind always scrambled to protect itself from anything new, even small things like trying to cut down my caffeine consumption, so this mammoth task was simply not computable.

The opportunity to grow and take on a new life was out there, but I was not ready for it yet. There was still other work that needed to be done.

And as I did it, and I continued to implement tweaks to improve my schedule, diet, and life, the clarity with which I saw the need to move to Canada became more and more.

Yet, I refused to listen.

It's too big!

Then, as you know by now, having exhausted all other options, and with my prevailing belief that there was meaning and purpose, I was put in a position that forced me to go.

I had left things to the last minute and had lost a lot of willpower. I was dazed and confused. I was humbled by my inability to change. But I retained my faith and hope.

Had I had the strength to change earlier, I may have been able to avoid this suffering. But the suffering came packed with necessary lessons, the biggest being to better listen to the messages that directed me where to go next in my life.

In short, I learnt to better listen to myself.

The beauty really lies in the fact that I can now see that everything worked out exactly the way it should have, to teach me these lessons and enable me to prove to myself that I could grow. And I did!

We all have an opportunity and the duty to unpack our past and use the wisdom achieved through this process to fuel our personal growth.

This reminds me of a story a wise, but also flawed, man once told me. He said that the answer to every question I would ever ask about myself could be found in my shadow. The simple truth could be deduced and explored by confronting what followed my every step. All wisdom could be rediscovered in the faded but ever-attached remnants of the past. This man spent 40 years dutifully unpacking his emotional backpack, and over that time, undid many externally and self-imposed sufferings. Eventually, he even dislodged the pain associated with the multiple abuses he had experienced as a child.

Although the man had worked hard all his life to do what he believed was right, he also unfortunately passed a portion of the pain in his backpack to his children. Largely, to his two sons. Both of whom had to carry this extra pain in addition to theirs. The extra pain caused many rifts between his sons, as well as the family, and made them turn against him.

Yet, he also passed on one lesson that saw them through. Both eventually turned and faced their shadow, both started to unpack the suffering in their emotional backpacks, and over time, peace was eventually restored in the family.

The man stands as a testament to the success that emerges from unpacking our pain. Although in a perfect world, he would not have passed his pain on, the suffering his sons and family inherited would have been far more destructive had he not made the decision to unpack.

How do I know this man so intimately?

That man is the king of the lions.

A man who has unpacked most of what once existed in his emotional backpack.

A man who will keep unpacking till his last breath.

A man I'm pleased to call my dad.

THE KEY TAKEAWAY

- We carry around our unacknowledged pain, in the form of our suffering, in an emotional backpack. The human experience is set up such that if we miss a lesson, or simply ignore pain, then we will, at some point, have to face up to it once more. Often, in the form of a more difficult manifestation of the same problem. There is no running away forever. Within your backpack, lies the answer to why you get stuck in your life. Within your backpack, also hides the solution to all your problems. Rummage through this backpack. See what you find.

- Pain isn't an experience anyone would choose, especially if we have a choice to ignore it. But the longer we leave it in our backpack, the harder it becomes to eventually remove. The pain in our backpack manifests as suffering in our life. The less we understand why we are suffering in our life, the more likely it is that major things need to be removed from the emotional backpack.

- We can start to unpack our backpack through meditation and by developing a consciousness of the past's hold on our current lives. This process takes radical honesty and hinges completely on our patience. It takes time to unpack what is squashed at the bottom of our backpack.

AN EASY START TO UNPACKING OUR EMOTIONAL BACKPACK

An easy practice to begin, to better understand what is in our emotional backpack, entails completing the following emotional backpack exercise.

This emotional backpack exercise is simple. The objective is to start unpacking what is in our backpack. We must search our past with the curiosity of an explorer, not the criticism of a judge. We are merely attempting to gain an awareness of what is in our backpack. This starts with the easier things at the top and then, eventually, moves down to the far more difficult ones that we have long packed away.

Here are 7 easy steps for completing this exercise:

1. Draw a large rectangle on a piece of paper.

2. Separate this rectangle into 3 equal sections. Label the first section 'Easy – My last year', label the second 'Ok – My last 10 years', and label the last 'Hard – My entire life'.

3. This rectangle is where you will write short notes based on your meditations on this subject.

4. The question you will ask yourself during your mediations, to complete this exercise, is *"Who or what hurt me enough that I forgot who I was, where I was going, or what I was doing?"*

5. First, meditate on the 'Easy' answer and think about who hurt you in the last year.

6. Don't rush the process. If it takes you 3 or more mediation sessions to work through the pain from the last year, then take that time.

7. Once you have completed the 'Easy' section, move on to the 'Ok' section, and eventually, the 'Hard'.

Once we complete our meditations on all three sections, we will better understand what exists in our emotional backpack. We may not yet know how to directly overcome these issues, but awareness of them is always the first step to finding a solution.

For the process for mediation, there are 3 key steps we need to effectively meditate on this subject:

1. Gift yourself 20 minutes. Find a quiet place and sit or lie down in a comfortable position. Take a few deep breaths. Focus on your breathing. Do not ignore distractions as they come, instead let them merely wash over you. Once you are relaxed, advance to Step 2.

2. In a relaxed state, ask yourself, *"Who or what hurt me enough that I forgot who I was, where I was going, or what I was doing?"* Then wait and be patient! This process can take time. Just sitting with these questions is subconsciously helping you begin unpacking your past.

3. If you didn't 'hear' anything while meditating, DON'T WORRY. Just take the time to repeat Steps 1 and 2 weekly until something becomes clear. There is no rush.

NOTE: If this process is bringing up unmanageable emotions, then please contact a therapist or counsellor to help you unpack your past.

Chapter 6
Breathe in and Find your Gem

January 2015, Cusco, Peru

The altitude sickness had long gone, but the taste of coca tea remained. The leafy green lift lingered in my mouth as I lay comfortably on the uncomfortable mattress of my cheap hostel bed.

The events of the last few days played through my mind, like a celebratory showreel at an award ceremony.

The first cinematic shot showed me stepping out of the Alejandro Velasco Astete International airport at 5 o'clock in the morning. The camera panned across my tired eyes, unrested after the 24-hour journey from London and then lingered for a moment on my mouth, which slightly curved upwards with conviction. It showed my first encounter with the street dogs, my side-stepping the one that foamed at the mouth, and my eventual realization that the pack that followed me were in no way truly dangerous; that they were, in fact, welcoming me to their land. The clip showed my eventual discovery of a hostel, and my poor, but ultimately successful, attempt to book a room.

"¿Puedo reservar una cama?"

I blink, and my mental picture house transports me to my next moment.

I'm now standing tall, arms outstretched, with pride coursing through my veins. A wide-angle shot from miles below shows the peak of the Sun Gate, and then slowly zooms into my celebratory moment. Below me, the delicate stone weaves of Machu Picchu seem effortlessly etched onto the dramatic peaks of the Andean countryside. All remaining fear of heights has temporarily been dislodged by the adrenaline of conquer.

Blink.

I'm now sitting in the middle of a field, holding my breath, and quieting down my mind, willing that an alpaca would let her young wander closer to me. Hoping she will allow me to simply sit in the presence of the tiny, precious, bundle of fluff. A rogue white pixel on a screen of verdant green. The wind sweeps through the field's green fingers and carries my calm to the baby alpaca who treads tentatively towards me.

Blink.

I now see the beaming smile of Gloria, the custodian of the hut with the faded blue door. The door acting as the sole highlighting accent on the car-sized corrugated iron shack. I listen to but do not fully comprehend her words as she invites me to take a look inside. I feel a warmth emanating from her that I could not possibly imagine in the south London suburb I called home, where strangers are almost always preconceived an immediate threat.

Thump!

I was broken from my reverie by the sound of a heavy suitcase hitting the door of my cosy, temporary abode.

I sighed satisfied.

My trip to Peru had been a true revelation. I'd been gifted a brand-new perspective. I'd been given a new world view that would allow me, with time, to unshackle myself from my crippling self-limiting thoughts. From my panic surrounding the perceived scarcity of good things in the world to my fear of failure.

I admit that I felt a little guilty about how small-minded I'd been until then. How little of the world I knew and understood. How the accomplishments I was most proud of amounted to nothing more than a disjointed story here. How my pride seemed like nothing more than vanity in this light.

Gloria hadn't taken a shine to me, because I played music to big crowds, or because I worked a certain job, looked a certain way, or even because I deserved it. Gloria was unconditionally kind to me, because that is how she expected others to be when welcoming her.

What was most remarkable to me, at the time, was that Gloria was clearly far happier than I was. It is less remarkable to me now, as I realize that Gloria had been happy as she had chosen to be so. To her credit too. This was against far greater odds than I, yet I had still chosen to allow life the get me down. She had found her gem, her little truth, in the gratitude she displayed for what she had, and she was so grateful for the little that she did have, that she was happy to share it welcomingly with whoever crossed her path.

She was helping others understand how they could grow by simply being. She was living authentically.

I decided then and there, as the memories of the life-altering trip rushed past, that I needed to be a little more like Gloria. I needed to not only focus on emptying my emotional backpack but also on discovering what gems I could find to share with others. What little truths I could pick out that would help others avoid going through what I had.

I had once stood at the edge of a bridge, ready to jump and end my life. In the last few days, I had stood 8,924 ft over sea level, at the peak of the Sun Gate, and on that peak, the last thing I had wanted to do was fall. The journey from a near-death low to a new-life peak had been tough and littered with mistakes. I had learnt a lot of lessons the hard way.

I realized then that I had a choice. A choice that would forever alter the course of my life. The choice was between three options:

1. I could choose to live life focused on what had been, and live forever drowning in suffering, regret, and humiliation.

2. I could choose a life focused on what will come, and live with a perpetual fear of the unknown.

3. I could try to live life as it came. To enjoy things for what they are in the present, and to be grateful for what I have right now.

Simply, I had a choice to be either as I had been, a rough combination of options 1 and 2, or a little more like Gloria, an epitome of option 3.

I chose the latter.

A few months later, I wrote the lyrics to a song I recorded in my friend's studio. It was never released:

"I've been living in the future and that won't last,
Caught in the problems of the past
And that's no way to grow"

This song was an homage to the choice I had made. It was a promise to myself that I would consistently and constantly train my mind and body to live with more awareness of the present. This song was a vow that I would continue to unpack my heavy emotional backpack, until it was empty. This song was the start of the journey I would embark on next. A journey that led me, a little less than a year later, to make the somewhat snap decision to move to Canada.

It really was as simple as that. I needed to allow myself to grow by relinquishing both what had come before and that which may come next. Then, with my new centred state, I could absorb the wisdom I had uncovered on this journey and share it with as many people as I could, thereby not only validating my experience but also helping heal the world.

This was my gem. This would be my gift of truth to the world. A roadmap that I will eventually share with others to help them move from a state of turmoil to a state of peace. A roadmap that will act as a guide for getting out of ruts. A guide that will also allow people to realize and then choose to live up to their infinite potential. A promise that once I implement these learnings into my life, I would help others do so as well.

If you haven't gathered yet, you are currently reading the fulfilment of that very promise.

THE KEY TAKEAWAY:

• Once we've confronted our pain, and compassionately assessed it, we can find little gifts of truth in the darkness. These 'gems' are like roadmaps that can help others find the answer to the lesson you have learnt, without having to take as many detours as you did.

• Our gems can sometimes seem so obvious when examined, but the knowledge of how we uncovered them is fundamentally useful to people who are stuck where we once were.

• Our gems should be fully implemented in our lives before being shared with others. Gems that we share, the ones that aren't properly assimilated in our day to day life, can easily come across as hypocritical when shared. However, if properly implemented in our lives, these gems act as magnets drawing in people who need the answers that we have found.

• You don't need to actively go out of your way to do your gem justice. In fact, you merely need to embody it, learn from it, and shine with it.

AN EASY START TO FINDING YOUR GEM

An easy practice to get into, to help uncover your gems, is running through the following gem discovery exercise. This exercise builds upon the emotional backpack exercise and allows us to find beauty in the hardships we have endured.

Here are 5 easy steps for completing this exercise:

1.   Find and read through your Emotional Backpack sheet. Number each identified pain, starting with 1 and ending with whatever number you reach.

2.   Get another piece of paper. Draw a large rectangle on this fresh piece of paper.

3.   Separate this new rectangle into 3 equal sections. Label the first section 'Easy – Lessons from last year', label the second 'Ok – Lessons from my last 10 years', and label the last 'Hard – Lessons from my whole life'.

4.   This rectangle is where you will write short notes based on your reflection on this subject.

5. The question you will ask yourself during this thought process is, *"What did I learn from each of these numbered pains?"* And subsequently, *"What lessons could I teach others to help them not have to face what I faced?"*

6. First, think through the 'Easy' pains and identify your lessons learnt in the last year, the little truths otherwise known as your gems.

7. Don't rush the process. If it takes you three or more sessions to work through the pain in the last year, then take all that time.

8. Once you have completed the 'Easy' section, move onto the 'Ok' section, and eventually, the 'Hard'.

For the process of thinking through this, there are 3 key steps we need to effectively reflect on this subject:

1. The first step to uncovering our 'gems' is to accept that we were wronged, hurt, or that we ourselves make mistakes. In accepting this, we can view the past in a new light.

2. The second step is to think about how you could advise someone else to overcome the same problem you faced. *e.g. if your pain surrounds the feeling that you are a failure, because you never felt you could impress your dad. You could advise someone that they have nothing to prove to anyone but themselves – not even their family!*

3. The third and final step is to be grateful for the lesson that you've learnt. The gem you've dug out, by compassionately understanding the pain of the past and learning from it, is a valuable gift to anyone who faces a similar problem to the one you overcame.

Chapter 7
Ignite through Expression
November 2013, Montreal, Canada

We weren't seeing eye to eye that day and we hadn't been for a very long time. There was no denying it. I was coming out of my shell regarding my gender identity, sexuality, and was exploring myself through open-ended spirituality. Meanwhile, his path led him on a thirsty quest for knowledge through tireless fact-checking and debate, which had, *at this point in time*, brought him to an appreciation of Catholicism.

The irony was that although we both saw each other as pig-headed ignorant fools, we were both on the exact same journey. We were both forging an identity for ourselves, we were both attempting to unpack our emotional backpacks, and we were both trying our best.

As philosophical thinkers and truly sensitive people, we had both become masters of our ends of the unhealthy debate. We regularly engaged in conversations of perceived purpose, which devolved into shouting matches over who had arrived at the truth. Looking back, I now realize that neither of us was even close to any truth, however hard we may have been looking for it.

Either way, lumping ourselves together for a lengthy retreat, on an entirely different continent, with a Jesuit priest as a mediator may not have been the wisest of ideas.

But that is exactly what happened.

Me, my younger brother, and the priest. I was all too aware that my life was starting to sound like a joke.

We had been feuding for years, endlessly pontificating, and always on the lookout for point-scoring opportunities. Within a day or two of us being on the retreat, the priest had advocated for the introduction of alcohol into our proceedings. I will never know whether this was a bid to help build some sort of camaraderie amongst us or just to lighten the mood. In reality, it sharpened our tongues and our scathing words sliced even deeper.

The priest remained a wise man, but nothing could help at this point. Soon, he realized this too and tried instead to work with us individually. We were too personally broken to fix our relationship.

Over a short call home, when my mum asked how things were going, I said, "We are never going to figure this out".

We'd both lost faith.

But right when things were beginning to look totally helpless, something interesting happened.

The day that things changed had been like all others on the retreat. The flurries of Montreal snow, the short walk to the grocery store to buy a smoked salmon wrap, and the simmering resentment between me and my brother. Close to boiling point.

That day was when things became truly explosive.

We'd spent the afternoon in the living room, viciously arguing the virtues, or lack thereof, of organized religion. Aggressive energy engulfed us, as we both raged self-righteously. Soon we broke into a fight. That's when things got very personal. Personal to the point where I felt tears stinging my eyes. Personal to the point where I had to retreat . . . from the retreat.

I ran to my room, locked the door, grabbed my guitar, and slumped on the bed. I didn't plan a single word, nor write any lyrics. Drowning in emotion, I just started playing.

Then something magical happened.

I realized that words were flowing from my mouth, but I did not have to think about it. I realized too that the ideal chord progressions were slipping through my fingers to the reverberating strings without my command. I was channelling something, and it was very raw.

I sang.

> '... and still you,
> You say I'm your brother, and I,
> I feel like another, and you.
> You never listen,

Even when I say it's ok.
It's ok'

The song didn't come from me, it flowed through me. I was merely an instrument of performance. Much like my guitar.

'I tried to teach you all that's good,
You turned to me and said I should,
Bend my knee to pray'

By the end of the experience, I was overwhelmed by only one thought, I had to record this down somehow. Wherever it came from, this magical song was surely supremely important.

I set up my laptop to record a video and sang the whole thing once more. Intuitively accepting the words, letting them flow from my mouth, and allowing my fingers to move where they had to.

Looking back now, I think just how amazing it is that I remembered every single lyric the second time through. Even though, I had never written them down, nor sang this song more than once, I knew exactly how it went. I look back and realize that my words had been a pure and resonant expression of a gem that I was in the process of uncovering at the time.

This was the gem of individual reality. The gem that allows us to see that our subjective view of the world is not truth, rather a projection of our inner being reflected at us. Had I understood this gem at the time, I would never have tried to impose my subjective view of the world on my brother, I would have merely accepted him for his reality, his view, and instead tried to put myself in his headspace. Not to join him, but to learn how to love him on his terms. Not mine.

This gem would have rendered our arguments obsolete. This gem would have allowed us to accept each other for exactly where we were on our individual life paths. And this gem would have brought about peace.

But it was not time yet. The retreat ended, and little seemed resolved. We both returned to England, drained.

A few weeks later I was in a studio on the south coast of England, recording that very song. A week or so following that, I had assembled a team to shoot a video. Every person involved in the video, somewhat incredibly, appeared on the scene just when they were needed.

A week later, the video was released to little fanfare.

Three months after that, I received an email. It read:

"Frankie

I'm sure you get this a lot, but your song changed my life.

I hadn't spoken to my brother for over 20 years before listening to your song, but since listening to it I took the plunge.
We have started working through our issues.
I just wanted say thanks."

That was the first time I'd ever been approached by a stranger telling me that something I created had changed their life. Let alone change it for the better.

From my pain and authentic expression, blossomed a healing opportunity for another human being. I helped someone have a better life. I helped heal the world in a little tiny way.

It felt good, so good, in fact, that it planted a new seed in my mind. The seed of radical honesty through expression. I realized then that by being open about our pain and our lessons, using whatever expressive form works best for us, we can help others. That it is in the expression of our gems through creative means, that we are able to affect the world for the better.

I made a promise to myself that I would nurture this seed into something beautiful. I was determined that this seed would blossom into a tree that sheltered people from the storms in their lives, a tree that converted the carbon dioxide of stress and pain into the oxygen of fresh life, a tree that would stand proud long after I'd left my body.

A few years later, I was sitting by a dramatically large window, in a high-end grocery store, snacking on a freshly prepared fart-inducing three-bean salad. I was back in Canada, planning my upcoming move.

Outside, the whistling wind whooshed with force, gripping leaves into its mighty puppeteer's grasp. I watched as they danced to its command, both unable to resist its clasp and also lovingly submitting to its allure.

As I appreciated the simple beauty of nature's show, I noticed a businessman stride past completely oblivious. He was on his phone, lost in a world of reports, projections, and quarters. Deeply, deeply detached from his surroundings.

I thought about how sad this was and wondered whether it was time to start expressing these daily little moments of clarity more openly. I could probably make a project of noting them down. Who knows, maybe this could be useful to someone. I made a solemn promise to myself, then and there, that I would write a poem, short story, or inspirational thought every single day, for an entire year.

365 days in a row. 365 teeny celebrations of the little clarity I found every day.

As I watched a woman struggle to carry her many bags, bullied by an updraft, I took my phone out and wrote an about-me paragraph for my project. To make it real.

It read:

*"The world is constructed from atomic particles that
are 99.999999999999% empty space. I write about what
exists in this space.*

*I am a Canadian-born, London-bred, nomadic soul
that shines brightest when exploring the world and
meeting its inhabitants".*

I made a website, crafted a pen name, and published
this about-me section the very next day.

365 days later, I had published 365 pieces of creative
writing. In celebration, I posted this poem:

> *'It seemed a mammoth task back then,*
> *A tall, tough, mountain challenge when,*
> *I stood a shrunken size.*
> *Yet now, I stand upon the peak,*
> *I see in all reality,*
> *That I am merely one step on,*
> *A journey that has just begun'*

In fact, after reaching my goal, I went on to write another 78 poems over the following 78 days.

My final entry was fitting, it was about the ever-changing nature of our life:

> *Our cells are never same,*

From day to day,
Nor are,
Our days.

I did not mince my words, nor speak inauthentically, for the 443 days that this project lasted. If I had a bad day, I spoke about it. If I had a great day, I spoke about that too. As a result, I had countless messages from people who could all relate to my experiences.

The beauty in both these examples, my song to my brother and my 443 poems, lies with these creative mediums doing all the heavy lifting. I didn't actually have to tell anyone what to do.

I could just focus on creating authentically, with the knowledge that as long as something resonated deeply within me, it might also resonate similarly in someone else.

Buoyed by the messages I was receiving for my poems, I was motivated to write an extended essay. The theme of the work was simple, it outlined how we are all born perfectly awesome, showcased the corrupting journey we all make as we grow up, and explained how I chose to set myself the challenge to return to how awesome I was at the beginning. One month after publishing the essay, as an extended online article, my mum and I went out for a coffee, this was the first time in my adult life. She spoke about how my essay had resonated with her, and she opened up to me about some of the trauma in her childhood. Six months later, she attended a retreat for those healing from challenging childhoods. Some 6 months beyond that, the course was such a resounding success for my mum, my dad decided to attend too.

Both have healed a great deal. Through their own strength, courage, and perseverance. My essay was not that important in the grand scheme of their transformation, but it did act as a small nudge in the right direction for my mum.

We don't need to tell people what can be done to help themselves, we can however have a far deeper and more lasting impact on their lives merely by showcasing our learnt lessons creatively.

No one likes to be told what to do. But we do love to be helped, assisted, and inspired by art, literature, and any other creative source that throws hints at us for how to overcome the ruts we are in. Or indeed, how to build our best life.

This is why I am recounting personal anecdotes in this book and not writing a rulebook for transformation. I hope that my stories will resonate in a way that rules simply can't.

There are no real 'rules', when it comes to life. Only pitfalls, gems, and the creative means you choose to express them.

THE KEY TAKEAWAY

• Although it isn't wise to tell people what to do, this does not mean that we must keep our gems to ourselves.

• We don't like being directly told what to do, this inhibits our sense of personal freedom. That said, we do all have that movie, song, poem, book, or painting that resonates with us so deeply that it fills us with emotion. We all love the expression of other people's gems through art and creative outlets. We just don't like being told "Do this!"

• We are all inherently creative, and although we may not have found our place in the more traditional arts, there are plenty of other ways to express our gems. Be it through an analogy we use in conversation, like the emotional backpack, or through our actions, like expressing the gem of unconditional kindness by giving a homeless person $10. We can all express our gems every single day that we live.

• Those who have found true peace and contentment in their lives realize that their gems are their greatest asset. They shine with these authentically and know that their entire life is a work of art. Their existence is an expression, and they, as master artists, can paint whatever they wish on the infinite canvas that is reality.

• It doesn't matter what the creative outcome is, whether you become a master painter or someone who chooses to walk along a beach collecting litter. What matters is that you express your gems.

AN EASY START TO EXPRESSING YOUR GEM

An easy place to start, when looking for ways to better express your gems, is to attempt the gem expression exercise. This exercise builds on the gem discovery exercise.

Here are 5 easy steps for completing this exercise:

1.   Find and read carefully your Gem Discovery sheet. Number each gem starting with 1 and ending with whatever number you have reached. It can be that all the hurt amounts to only one gem. Do not worry if this is the case, one authentically expressed gem is far more powerful than a hundred insignificant ones.

2.   Take another piece of paper. Draw a circle for each gem you have uncovered. *e.g. You should never let*

other people assign your personal worth to you. Only you can determine that.

3. For each gem then, think through different ways that you can express this gem in your life. Be as creative as you can and think as far outside the box as you can. *e.g. I could write my daughter a poem to explain this to her OR I could create an app that offers daily exercises to help people build better notions of self-worth OR I could come up with an analogy I can use to explain this to people when I think they could find this gem useful.*

If this process is proving difficult, then the following thought exercise will help you better understand the power of your gem as well as the way you can use it.

1. Know that your gem, however small, is a valuable resource to anyone who is going through the same situation as you. You are a pioneering explorer to them, one who is farther up the mountain they are trying to climb.

2. Get a pen and paper and write a letter to your past self, explaining how everything turned out ok, no

matter how hard things got. Also explain what you learnt and how you will avoid similar situations moving forwards. Keep it simple.

3. Once the letter is complete, summarize it as one simple finding. *e.g. "You should never let anyone tell you that you aren't good enough, not even your family"* This sentence is your gem to express. You can then express this in any way you wish. Artistically, creatively, or simply in the flow of conversation.

Chapter 8
Ignite with a life challenge

June 2012, London, England

What am I going to do?

I was sitting in silence, on the worn living room couch of my parent's front room, my hands draped lifelessly on my laptop's keyboard. I glance out of the window, expectantly, as if clarity on what to do next would materialize into existence at any moment in the garden.

It did not.

Instead, I saw the growing rust on the swing set, the uneven paving of the patio, and noticed the remarkable lack of anything to note. No birds, no insects, no vibrancy, and no . . . no life. All that existed beyond the window pane seemed stripped of joy by the melancholy glaze of the sunless sky.

I returned my gaze to my laptop's dim screen.

What next?

The prison radio gig had run its course, and I was once more unemployed, living with growing debt, and at a complete loss of clarity for the next steps I had to take. Had I been of a stronger spirit, I would have been searching for an exciting new adventure. But in my current state, I would be happy to find anything that could help

101

stop me from sliding back down into the pit I'd managed to begin clambering out of.

I need something. Anything. I'm desperate!

My daily search on the local job listings had given me no reason to smile yet, let alone celebrate. And I wasn't confident that something would come anytime soon. I felt directionless.

My mum, a very strong empath, had sensed this and taken me aside a few days earlier. She said, "If you don't know what to do, do something to help someone else".

Continuing, she said, "If you can't help yourself, then help someone else".

At the time I hadn't really understood what she was getting at, but in hindsight, I realize that she was simply saying that it is in helping others that we learn how to better help ourselves. My mind though, at the time, had simply clung to the notion that this may be a path to finding something that can help me not slump back into my suicidal depression.

Help others.

I was yet to take her advice literally and had been growing impatient. So, I started a new search on the job site I had been ignoring for the last five minutes. I typed,

'help others'

I hit enter.

The slow loading speed of our basic internet gave me a moment to revel in the stupidity of this act. At least I could make a joke about this with my mum.

"Turns out you really can't find a job helping people . . . Who knew? Ha ha!"

To my surprise though, I did find a smattering of results. I quickly scrolled through them to realize that I was unqualified for all but one. The remaining job posting was from a special needs school, and the role they were recruiting for was that of a carer and educator of severely autistic young adults aged 17–25.

You can't do this. You don't know the first thing about autism.

It was not my dream job, nor was it something that I had ever thought I would be good at. It did not pay well. And I would have to travel an hour and a half every day to get to the school. I was not enthused by the prospect. At all. There was no reason for me to take it.

But then, I couldn't travel back into the dark, and I trusted my mum's words. Perhaps . . . I could help these young adults. Perhaps, I would feel good about it.

Unlikely.

I applied, fully expecting to be rejected.

A week later, I was called in for an interview and a tour of the facilities. Shortly after, I was offered the job. I took it.

Getting out of bed, in the morning, on my first day, was a real test of courage. Having visited the school, for my tour, I had briefly seen the class I would be working with. The class had one carer for every two students and was described by the teacher I met in the corridor as 'hard work'. I assumed that hard work for someone as qualified as this teacher, would probably make for nearly impossible work for me.

You are going to fuck this up. Just stay in bed.

By the time I was on the train, I had become aware of a tension that was slowly gripping me. By the time I saw the school, I was ready to just run away and never come back. By the time I made it to classroom, which was right at the end of a long corridor, I thought I might be sick.

The first hour was petrifying. I felt the same panic you feel when holding a new-born baby...

Don't drop the baby! Don't drop the baby!

By hour two, I had already experienced my first adult diaper change and had been vomited on. I was questioning why the hell I thought I could do this.

I told you so!

But I persevered, and by lunchtime, I had calmed down a little. On my walk to the corner store, which I'd been promised existed at the end of the next road, I wondered whether this was it. My life for ever and ever. But was I really helping people?

Helping, shmelping. You aren't doing any good.

Then I ate. Lunch was a hurried convenience store sandwich and a packet of over-seasoned peanuts.

The first thing I saw on my return from lunch was one of the students, whose mental growth had stopped around three years old, laying on his front in the middle of the classroom floor, rubbing his groin against it aggressively. Sexually.

I froze.

Nearby, two carers were attempting to act as a human shield between the unfolding event and their assigned students. The remaining carers shared uneasy gazes as they frantically tried to distract the remaining confused classmates.

I stood petrified at the door, until the ordeal was concluded.

"You'll get used to it, and they'll get used to puberty", the elder carer said lovingly, as she turned to address my feeble form at the door, "they really are great people. You just need to get used to the way they are", she concluded.

The words resonated with me, and I resolved myself to get familiarized with the way they are. As a result, the afternoon's tone was lighter. I was assigned, along with a handful of other carers, to a small group, and we were tasked with helping the students name a collection of plastic fruits and vegetables.

I was soon working with a girl, one-to-one. She suffered from both severe autism and physical disabilities. She guessed banana for every single plastic fruit or vegetable I held up, including the banana. Her expression scrunched when I didn't positively reinforce that a potato was a banana. It seemed to confuse her to no end. There was a helplessness in her, which I couldn't quite place. Something baby-like.

Something totally innocent.

This seems so unfair. Why should anyone be like this?

I could feel a lump forming in my throat.

She stared at me confused for yet another moment, and then, bored of the task, pushed off all the plastic food from the desk. An act that made her smirk.

I did not know what to do.

Nearby, I heard a joyful squeal, and the clatter of fake fruit on the floor, as another student had mimicked her.

"That's not what we do, is it? Not with Frankie", the young male carer to my right said softly. Almost parent-like.

As I picked up the inedible fruits and vegetables from the floor, I couldn't help but feel like a total amateur. These carers were truly talented.

The day was soon up, and I said my goodbyes hurriedly. I could feel a tidal wave of tears welling up inside me.

I restrained my emotions as well as I could on the journey home. But as soon as I walked through the front door, I rushed to my room and cried for half an hour. The whole experience had been so overwhelming that I felt like calling in the next morning and telling them I would never go back.

I wasn't entirely sure what had hurt me so deeply in that classroom. Perhaps, it was the helplessness of the whole situation. Or maybe, it was the fact that even with all of their collective health problems, these disabled young people laughed more than I did. Their laughter in the face of adversity seemed all too familiar. Just months before, I had been shocked at how much laughter rang in the prison.

I felt like there was still something very wrong with me. It niggled at me. I needed to figure this out. Soon.

When I returned the next morning, the lead carer took me aside and whispered, "I'm honestly rather surprised you're here. Why did you come back?"

A little taken aback by the in-your-face honesty, I mumbled my mum's words, which still swam shallow in my subconscious, "I . . . I want to help".

A warm smile spread across her face. She placed her hand on my shoulder and said, "Welcome". I reciprocated, smiling back at her.

"The first day is always the hardest, and more than half of our new carers never come in for a second", she continued, "I'm glad you did".

At that moment, I knew that I was on the right track, and I ended up lasting there for half a year more than she'd thought I would.

Six months in, one of the larger boys threw a table at my head in a display of incredible force. I was concussed and taken to hospital.

A few days later, when I met with the headmaster, I was asked if I would report this to the police or press charges. I said I would not, but I knew then, I was ready to move on.

As I said my goodbyes to the class, the thought that even though we'd spent six months together, most of the students would have soon forgotten I even existed couldn't escape me. A guilt swept over me at the thought of those who wouldn't. What would they think of me for abandoning them? So many people had already done so before me.

After I left the building for the last time, I didn't walk back straight to the train station. Instead, I sat in a nearby park. Something had been building up inside throughout this entire experience. A puzzle piece in the grander portrait of my life that still eluded me. The phantom piece that would finally explain what had truly brought me here.

What's the lesson I was supposed to learn?

It hit me a few hours later, when I was in the shower.

The young adults would forever live in the same way, have the same level of comprehension of life, enjoy the same highly limited opportunities, and endure the same confusion regarding potatoes and bananas.

They were, for all intents and purposes, in a rut. A never ending one. It wasn't even one of their choosing, nor was it one that they could, or would, ever escape.

Two challenges were being set in my mind as the warm water cascaded down my shoulders. Challenges that would define the rest of my life.

First, I vowed that I would find a way to show people just how blind they are to the beauty in their lives. Just how infinite their potential is. Just how much power they have over what they get from life.

This would be my life's work and purpose, my greatest challenge.

And second, and most importantly at that point, if I wanted to prove that the first point was achievable, I foremost needed to escape the rut I was in and turn my life around once more.

I was in need of a bigger transformation, a much bigger one, and the first step was to get out of my financial debt, which, at that point in time, was around £15,000. That became my new focus. The beauty of the challenge I had undertaken at the special needs school was that in my attempt to help others, I had actually helped myself in a truly formative way. I had stepped out of my comfort zone in a bid to expand. And as a result, I had expanded, no longer having the fear of jumping in the deep end and trying something new.

So, I found a new challenge to sink my teeth into. Via the introduction of a friend, I took up an unpaid gig, presenting a daily Indie & Rock Music radio show at a local station. I enjoyed this opportunity to talk about music and create fun segments. I had not presented anything of this nature on radio since having a weekly radio spot with my friend, back in university.

My debt amount didn't budge, but I smiled a little more now. That smile started a few conversations with the staff at the station, and soon, I was telling my life story to the CEO of the company.

It was then that I learnt that the company was also a media arbitrator in the digital media space. Being a music fan and impressed by the fact that I'd once made a career for myself in music, he offered me job on his sales team.

On the day I signed on the dotted line, he said, "Well, here we go then. Show me just how good you are". He was a trendy media type, who glided around the office on a little skateboard and had a penchant for electronic music.

Over the succeeding years, I worked hard and rarely ever stopped challenging myself. I have to admit though, that there were stints where I got a little too comfortable.

Four years later, on a different continent, I'd worked my way up to a directorial level. And here I was, managing senior relationships with major corporate clients. By this point, I'd long paid off my debt and had built up a comfortable nest egg.

But what do I say, I felt the itch again. I needed a new challenge.

I didn't scratch this itch until I heard a song that reminded me of my childhood and the lion game that my dad and I played.

This time, I was much more aware of what the confusion was. This time, I was way more open to where it is taking me. As I meditated on what to do next, I remembered the initial challenge I had set myself back in that shower, all those years ago:

To find a way to show people just how blind they are to the beauty in their lives, to help them realize just how infinite their potential is and see just how much power they have over what they get from life.

I had long escaped the rut that I had been in when I first conceived this challenge, but then, I had gotten stuck in another. I needed to take a risk. I needed to make a change. And, I needed to make it smoother and quicker than my transition in moving to Canada.

I needed to take the next bold step in my story, and this step would have to come as a huge leap of faith. A new type of jump, completely into the unknown. This leap was not one born from the fact that I had nothing going for me. In fact, I actually had a lot to lose. I would need to forgo my great income, lose my swanky rented condo, and make this jump without truly knowing what was to come.

I needed my mind totally onside for this one.

I started visualizing my life without a corporate job. I started meditating daily to give me strength. I saw myself living far more modestly. But smiling more often. I saw myself taking good care of my health and exercising more. I saw myself temporarily financially poorer. But far wealthier in the long run. I saw joy, I saw peace, and I saw the next step.

I took it.

Two years on I've launched my own business, I'm working remotely from wherever in the world interests me and I'm making music and creative content that I could have only dreamed of before. I am ever closer to accomplishing my life's work.

I am sure that I will soon need to take another leap. A step that will surely terrify me a little more. Challenge me a little more. And bring me closer yet to my lifelong aspiration of helping people.

This is how we all grow. This is how *you* will grow.

Remember, the thrilling quest on which I've embarked initially started with a giant, painful, and thoroughly crappy rut.

So if you're in one of those... lucky you!

THE KEY TAKEAWAY

• To continue growing in life, it is important to continuously challenge ourselves. As our mind-set evolves, we look after our health better, we allocate our time better, we unpack our emotional backpack, and we turn the gems uncovered into beautiful gifts to the world. We are offered opportunities to challenge ourselves, to ignite our lives, and to become truly healthy, wealthy, and useful to others.

• Discovering our life's challenge and work is a lasting way to develop a sense of true meaning. It is worth pursuing. We will need to take leaps of faith to find this challenge. We must prove ourselves worthy to take it on.

• You don't need to know how you will accomplish your challenges, but you do need to start working on them now. Not tomorrow. With clear focus on them every day, we start to see the world with a renewed vision. We start perceiving solutions where there were once only problems.

• If we take a moment daily to visualize what it would be like to achieve our dreams, we can help expedite the process. "What will I feel like when I've taken the leap? What will others say to me? What will my senses feel?"

• Challenges that focus on selfish motives of serving only ourselves tend to end in failure. The challenges that end in incredible success are almost always the ones that help many, many other people. Serving others, inspired and supported by our gems, is not only emotionally rewarding but also financially so. People pay for solutions to their problems. Solve their problems.

AN EASY START TO SETTING A LIFE CHALLENGE

An easy practice to get into, while trying to find one's life challenge or work, is attempting the following exercise.

1. List 5 things you want to achieve in your lifetime, OR List 5 ways you would like to see the world change. PICK ONE. The most important one.
2. Be mindful that we can't control the things life throws our way, but we can control the way we react to these. We can also make our life meaningful by working towards our big challenge.

3. Decide what you can do today, tomorrow, and every day for the rest of your life to work towards the CHALLENGE you have chosen. Small steps every day, leading to inevitable change.

Chapter 9
Celebrating Transformation

September 2017, London, England

It was a little surreal. But I had always known it would be when I finally returned.

Five years had seamlessly slipped by since we'd done our last show. Five years exploring different routes. On different quests – two of these we'd spent separated by the Atlantic Ocean. So much had changed, so many new stories had been written, and it was clear that we had both done a lot of growing up.

He has definitely been working out.

I spoke first, "Shall we listen to some of our previous song ideas then, for old time's sake?"

He smiled, "Sure Frank".

Only he has ever called me Frank and lived to tell the tale.

I feel a warmth wash over me as I lay down on the bed in his room. I was back in his family home, for the first time in a few years. It had been a home away from home for me. A sanctuary where he and I honed our musical craft. Although the decor had changed, the energy had stayed.

I'm home.

As he loaded the first of the old tracks, I thought of the generous embrace his mum had wrapped me in after a great conversation, catching up on my life in Canada. I remembered her words,

"You know that you are welcome here anytime, right? It's really lovely to see you".

I had spent so many of my formative years here. My mind danced with vivid memories, all good.

"Do you remember when we used to jam in your living room? Your mum was always so generous! Two guitars and a bass. And my screaming!" I said to my great friend.

"Yer", he says, smiling.

We were so naive then, all ready to take on the world.

He's never been a man of many words. I am. This dynamic has seen us write countless songs. I bring the words and melody. He brings the beat, the production, and the craft.

I'm so happy.

The first song blared out from his speakers, the lyrics hitting me deep.

'Never forget,
Always believe,
You are the runner and I am the seed,
Stand here together,
And you can see,
We're building and making

An empire to lead'

I remembered writing this!

"This was the song that made it on national radio, you remember man?" I ask him, reminiscing about the old times.

"Yer, it's actually pretty good", he replies, also lost in contemplation.

We spend the next hour flitting through songs and demos, from successful expressions to failed ideas. Some of our creative attempts could not withstand the test of time, whilst others transported us back to another world. A place so different to what we saw now. Particularly for me. A lot of these songs were written during my darkest days, and although I never directly addressed the issues in them, the essence remained.

I felt my eyes close slowly as if my whole body and being were reacquainting itself with these musical mementos.

Before I knew it, I had been transported back to that time. I remembered the biggest show I'd ever performed. The electrifying energy of the crowd. And the rush still hit me. Then, the scene shifted, and I remembered a few shows later, when I had drunk an entire bar-sized bottle of vodka, insulted the headlining act who had just had their first ever No 1 hit on the UK Charts that week, and then had tried to jump out of the van on the way home. I remembered the countless times my bandmate had supported me. How he had been there, when I cried almost every night after drinking. How he had given me his time, helping me work through my problems with music. The joy we had shared playing at festivals. The liberation of life on the road. The rock and the roll.

"You are the best, you know that, right?" I heard myself saying to him, whilst I was still floating in the haze of memory.

He laughed, "What . . . why?"

I snapped back to reality, "hmm? Oh. Because you are", I replied.

And then silence descended once more, as our next idea was loaded.

He clicked play.

As I slipped into the groove of the next track, I heard my past signing to me.

"And I'm floating so dangerously close to edge,
And I will fight it, but I'll never win"

As the waves of my past voice sank into my core, timelessly, I realized something beautiful.

I am no longer this person. I am better because of this experience. I am grateful for this experience.

This was in many ways a celebration. A celebration of my life. A party marking my triumph over personal adversity, and an ode to show compassion with oneself.

Another hour passed, as we sat reminiscing and healing. Then something stopped me in my tracks.

"You remember the song that we wrote that went like . . ." I said excitedly, proceeding to hum it.

The last note was met by silence.

"So . . . You know?" I asked.

"Seems familiar", he said, scrunching his brow, and we set about finding it.

Luckily, we'd just spent the last 2 hours browsing through our deep historical catalogue of attempts at forming the perfect song. Unluckily, we had around 150 project files worth of music. We had made a large dent. But there still remained plenty to listen to.

We have to find it. There's something there.

Another half hour passed, and we started to lose a little hope. Perhaps, this song was long lost on an old harddrive. Perhaps, it had been deleted. Perhaps . . . And then one small, deeply meaningful, click of the mouse started the next chapter of our musical journey.

The first few notes rang out.

This is it!

I sat up on the bed and squealed, "This is the one!"

"Yer", he smiled, then we both listened in quiet excitement.

As the next 3 minutes passed, we both quickly realized that the song is steeped in real potential. A potential that we could not let go of. We spent the next 4 hours tweaking the synths, the beat and recording new vocal ideas.

And that was that.

I said goodbye to my old friend, to his mother, to the house where some truly great memories lived. And I hopped on a plane back over the Atlantic.

The song we had found and re-written tucked away a little magic in it. Something really special. Within a few weeks of my return to Canada, I'd found a truly inspiring actor to start scripting a music video with. Then, the perfect choreographer two-stepped his way in. A wonderful cinematographer appeared. A top class editor. Some wonderful local fashion designers drew us some really gorgeous looks. The ideal venue materialized. A crew assembled. A makeup artist was hired. A troupe of four professional dancers sauntered in. And friends offered to act as PAs.

Everything was coming together like never before. Plus, due to my corporate stint, I now had a little money saved to dedicate to the project. On leaving the corporate world, I'd promised to spend my savings (albeit quite modest) pursuing my art and creativity, and I felt so alive to be actually doing it. I was far less fearful than I had anticipated.

The video was, and remains, an absolute celebration of all that we had worked on. A true triumph.

But, celebrations are not something I reserve solely for times like this. Celebrations are a way of life, much like happiness. It is a choice. It is what we can choose every single day.

A true celebration of life is only achievable when you realize that today, this day, may indeed be your last. There are no promises, no guarantees, that we will live on beyond our next sleep. There are no pacts. Nor omniscient clarity.

Whether we celebrate through our artistic expression or solely through our joyful actions, life shines with a whole new brightness when we are looking at it as one big celebration.

THE KEY TAKEAWAY

• When we think of celebrating, we think of achieving big goals, winning in a major way, or ultimate victory. But wouldn't it be great if we could celebrate the smaller things? Or rather, just celebrate being here? In doing so, we would be able to live much happier lives.

• The reality is that, much like happiness, we must choose to celebrate our lives for what they are. We must choose to show gratitude for the smaller things. We must choose to see all the beauty that is around us.

AN EASY START TO CELEBRATING OUR LIVES

An easy practice to get into, when trying to celebrate more is to:

1. Gift yourself 1 minute. Force yourself to smile. Pull the widest smile you possibly can, and keep smiling until you laugh. Smiling every day, no matter how we feel, lifts our mood and alleviates some stress. It is physiologically proven that smiling does make you happier. SMILE NOW. SMILE OFTEN.

2. Plan 3 ways you can celebrate your life every week, and schedule adequate time to do these 3 things.

Here are some simple examples:

- I will celebrate the great things in my life by writing down 5 things that I take for granted, which not everyone in the world is lucky enough to have.

- I will celebrate my life, especially my body, by taking part in a physical activity that I truly enjoy.

- I will celebrate my life by telling 5 close friends how special they are to me.

- I will celebrate my life by reading a great and inspiring biography of someone I revere.

Chapter 10: Failure isn't just an option, it's the way

How many times did you fall flat on your ass as a toddler learning how to walk? 10? 100? 1000? Either way, it happened a lot. It happened frequently. And it was a part of your everyday life.

Ouch!

How bruised your booty ended up being is not the point here. Rather how many times you failed and then picked yourself up again is. The ingrained perseverance of your young, unadulterated mind. The natural sense of knowing that you would eventually succeed. Had you given up after the 999th fail, you would still be crawling today. But you failed your way to inevitable success.

You were once a phenomenal success. A being who understood that success comes only after a series of failed attempts. A wonderful, fearless explorer of new lands. A winner.

Then, you were taught that failure is the absolute worst thing possible. That failure is not an option. That failure must be avoided at all costs. So instead of trying to succeed, you turned your focus and learnt how to be wonderfully adept at avoiding failure.

127

You always win the game you are playing. The game you are playing is called "not losing". Why not play a game called winning? The risk may seem higher, but the rewards make it much more worthwhile!

And I admit that growth is scary. Transformation is a huge challenge. And you will fall off track.

Why? Because oftentimes, the pull of old ways is stronger than the push of our new drive. You will fall off track. You will fail, and you will lose. This is a part and parcel of the journey.

So when your new fitness habit, your new scheduled time to do something you love, or your weekly gem discovery process is disrupted by something that simply cannot go unaddressed, FEAR NOT! Each stumble, each fall, and each unavoidable step off course is only part of the process of failing your way to success.

In fact, successful people often celebrate their moments of failure, or at the very least, feel the blow lessened by the simple reality that their recent failure is a sign that they have never been closer to success.   The most successful people also know how crucial it is to have contingency plans for failures. To realize the inevitability of life's distractions, and to account for the obstacles and stumbles that will almost certainly cross our path.

We were born with the knowledge that failure is an intrinsic part of the route to lasting success. And as we realized this, we didn't stop trying to walk, or speak, or even

128

write, when we had failed the hundreds of times previously.

Somewhere down the line, while growing up, we became more afraid of failure than excited about success. But know this . . .

Failure isn't an option, it's just the way.

Life is a raging river with wild rapids, and you are in a dinghy. Unless you learn to go with the flow, you will thrash wildly at the water with your paddle, hoping, in vain, that by doing so, you may be able to gain some sort of control over your course.

Moreover, you are always second-guessing your true route. And as a result, you aren't taking any consistent actions to aim yourself one way or another. You frantically follow whatever path seems the calmest at the time. But as a fallible human like the best of us, you often fail to pick the right route.

As a result of your interference, you often end up crashed against rocks or fallen logs and start feeling like you will never be able to reach the calmer waters downstream.

I feel your frustration. I've been there many times.

During these times, it is important to uncover the ways in which we can improve ourselves, our actions, and how we can work on optimizing the way we live. It is important to take the reins within ourselves, it is the only thing we can truly control.

Then, taking a moment to breathe, we are able to plan a route away from that which has impeded us. We now confront our fear of capsizing and boldly push away from what is in our way, and navigate skilfully around it.

Once we have reached a calmer stretch, and before going for the next wild ride, it is also important to look back and understand what we've learnt. From this vantage point, we have wisdom that can be shared with those further upstream. Wisdom that can help them navigate the waters we just faced, only far more tactfully.

And then we float on, paddling a little less frantically, having let go of our need to control the river quite so much, instead working harder on ourselves, and bathed in a new magnanimity.

We start to bob along.

And then up ahead, we spot the next wild ride, the next fallen log, and we are a little more prepared than we were before.

And that, my friends, is what we call life.

An exercise in escaping ruts and reaching towards something better.

Printed in Great Britain
by Amazon